Steven,
We Need to Talk

*A DNA Journey That Led Me to an
Unexpected and Wonderful New Family*

Why a decision to do DNA testing was my right thing to do.

Steven Vermeulen

Copyright © 2019 Steven J Vermeulen and Melody K Vermeulen.

All rights reserved. No part of this book may be reproduced, stored, or transmitted by any means—whether auditory, graphic, mechanical, or electronic—without written permission of the author, except in the case of brief excerpts used in critical articles and reviews. Unauthorized reproduction of any part of this work is illegal and is punishable by law.

This book is a work of non-fiction. Unless otherwise noted, the author and the publisher make no explicit guarantees as to the accuracy of the information contained in this book and in some cases, names of people and places have been altered to protect their privacy.

ISBN: 978-1-4834-9902-4 (sc)
ISBN: 978-1-4834-9903-1 (hc)
ISBN: 978-1-4834-9901-7 (e)

Library of Congress Control Number: 2019903072

Because of the dynamic nature of the Internet, any web addresses or links contained in this book may have changed since publication and may no longer be valid. The views expressed in this work are solely those of the author and do not necessarily reflect the views of the publisher, and the publisher hereby disclaims any responsibility for them.

Any people depicted in stock imagery provided by Getty Images are models, and such images are being used for illustrative purposes only. Certain stock imagery © Getty Images.

Lulu Publishing Services rev. date: 03/28/2019

*Dedicated to everyone searching for
family and seeking answers.*

*Never stop trying.
Never stop believing.
Never give up on the journey.
When we have family, we are never alone in life.*

Family
Life's Greatest Gift

Contents

Special Acknowledgments ix
Preface xi
Introduction xiii

Chapter 1:   My Early Years 1
Chapter 2:   My Preteen and Early Teen Years 7
Chapter 3:   When Ignorance and Intolerance Came Calling 10
Chapter 4:   Our Family Business Forms 13
Chapter 5:   My High School Years 16
Chapter 6:   My First Taste of Real Freedom 19
Chapter 7:   Steven, We Need to Talk 22
Chapter 8:   My Name Is What? 26
Chapter 9:   My Search Begins 29
Chapter 10: A Father and Family Are Found 33
Chapter 11: I Think I Found My Brother 35
Chapter 12: Spitting in a Tube 37
Chapter 13: Weeks? 41
Chapter 14: I'm Getting Close 44
Chapter 15: Steven, We Need to Talk (Again) 46
Chapter 16: I Follow the Bread Crumbs 49
Chapter 17: Questions, Questions, Questions 52
Chapter 18: Wrestling with Answers 56
Chapter 19: Dad, Is That You? 59
Chapter 20: I Ask Myself More Questions 62
Chapter 21: A Sibling Responds 64
Chapter 22: We Begin Telling Friends and Family 66
Chapter 23: We Must Get Together 70
Chapter 24: Meeting Time Has Arrived! 73
Chapter 25: After Sixty-One Years, Father and Son Meet at Last 76

Chapter 26: Oh No, Surely Not 79
Chapter 27: Honoring a Life Well Lived 81
Chapter 28: Family Fellowship and Future Plans 84
Chapter 29: The Siblings Are Gathered 87
Chapter 30: Two DNA Services Agree 88
Chapter 31: Positive Notes 89
Chapter 32: The Best Accidental Family One Could Ask For 91
Chapter 33: Collateral Damage? 93
Chapter 34: New Family, Old Traditions 95
Chapter 35: Melody 98
Chapter 36: Janelle 102
Chapter 37: Ellon 105
Chapter 38: Denise 107
Chapter 39: Chuck 113
Chapter 40: Cheryl 122
Chapter 41: Debra 126
Chapter 42: Janel 128

Epilogue 131
My Journey 134
My Siblings 135
Submitting Your DNA 137
The Moral of This Story 139
In Conclusion 141
About the Author 145

Special Acknowledgments

It is hard to know where to begin when thanking everyone for their help and personal contributions in making this story come to life. This book could not have become a reality without the support and encouragement of our family and friends.

Melody and I wish to give our very special thanks to:

Denise, Chuck, Cheryl, Debra, and **Janel** for being so instantly welcoming to a brother who literally popped up out of nowhere.

Ellon Weeks for her incredible acceptance, kindness, and understanding when I came into the family.

Theresa Olande for helping me identify the DNA link between myself and the Weeks family whom Melody and I have come to love so much.

Denise Weeks Lovell who was the first to suggest we should write a book in hopes it would help others.

Janelle Ballard for being there for me throughout this journey just as she has been there for me throughout our lives.

Peggy Garner Ballard for the awesome book title she suggested.

Amie Horan for her countless hours of editorial help, expertise, and cover design.

Our **closest friends** and **family** who have shared in our wonder and excitement this past year and let us talk their ears off so often about the wonderful outcome.

Last, and certainly not least, my mother, **Connie Vermeulen**, for being willing to finally let go of her most closely guarded secret and providing me the details of how this all came to happen. I know it was not easy for her to tell the truth of my origin, but I am so grateful she found the courage.

Preface

What would you think if you made a seemingly innocent request for a copy of your birth certificate at age nineteen only to have your mother reveal to you that your family relationships were not as you had been told throughout your life? What deep secrets can be hidden within that simple document? What would you think if your mother told you forty years later that she had not been truthful the first time she provided that specific information? Can you lose and gain a family more than once in a lifetime?

After experiencing the first revelation about who my "real" father was when I reached my late teens, my life turned in a new direction. I began a long and partially successful journey to find my birth father and paternal relatives. As my search progressed during the next several years, information was often difficult to find until technology began to play a more significant role in resource availability. Much later in my life, while trying to find one specific person identified by my mother as a biological half-brother, a second revelation landed in my lap like a bombshell.

Following completion of DNA testing that had not been available in those earlier years, a question arose when the results did not match long-held knowledge of my father's name or family. Where I had failed in one searching aspect, I would succeed in many, many others. However, with triumph, unfortunately, often comes tragedy. How you deal with both is a testament to your character, perseverance, and resilience.

This is the story about my journey to find my biological father and his family and the reasons why I undertook it. It involved countless twists and turns as the search led to many a dead end. Through advancements in technology, the journey reached a wonderful and amazing outcome that I now joyously get to live.

This story and my journey would not have been possible without the assistance of my wife, Melody. She was instrumental in helping me through the many years of research and provided emotional support when I became frustrated or sullen by the lack of progress as I pursued the unknown.

With the constant and endearing encouragement from friends and family once this writing began, this story has gone through many iterations as I dared to share more and deeper personal information and circumstances. I want to thank everyone involved for their patience with my numerous draft copies, the constant badgering for review, and their ever-so-thoughtful suggestions about things they would like to see included, expanded upon, edited, or excluded.

Introduction

Hello. I grew up believing my name was Steve Vermeulen. I will explain that statement in detail throughout this story.

I was born in January 1956 in Hyannis, Cape Cod, Massachusetts. I undertook my DNA journey in hopes of finding a half-brother I believed was just a few months younger than me. It has led to the incredible discovery of an awesome family I had no idea existed until July 2017. The journey that started in 1975 included hope, anticipation, trepidation, love, and tragedy.

I heartily recommend that anyone who starts this kind of journey keep an open mind and an open heart and be ready to accept and embrace the wonders that could be presented. Be understanding and considerate of the circumstances of all parties involved, yet never be fearful of finding the truth. Most importantly, understand your reasons for taking the journey and share those generously with your contacts. Let them into your world before you ask to join theirs.

CHAPTER 1

My Early Years

My earliest memories are from after we moved from Cape Cod to Des Moines, Iowa, where I lived from the age of two into early adulthood. Growing up in Iowa was generally good. There was city life and amenities surrounded by vast open areas that led to opportunities for growth and experiences of all varieties.

My family consisted of my mother, Connie; my dad, Moe; my three sisters; and me. Kerry was born in December 1954, Janelle was born in December 1957, and Brenda was born in August 1962. I was the second child and the only boy. Being the sole boy was key to my upbringing. It gave me more responsibility, but also afforded me much more freedom than my sisters were allowed. The freedom was a way of life in the old-fashioned values held by my dad and his family.

I learned to fish, hunt, camp, handle dogs, and work hard during my early years. The work part was generally hard labor. It included building sheds and garages, remodeling the house, pouring concrete, laying brick and stone, shoveling snow, mowing, gardening, trimming trees, raising dogs (a kennel operation), and so on. You know, all those things a small child should be doing!

There was a lot of playtime in the summers while Dad was at work and Mom was busy with the house. Weekdays after Dad came home from his job with the City of Des Moines Housing Code Inspection and Enforcement Division, my daily life changed to the role of his Boy Friday as I would assist him with whatever his daily plans entailed. Weekend days were spent hanging out with Dad and continuing to act as his full-time assistant. Just as I spent time working with my dad, my sisters spent time acting as full-time assistants to our mother.

Our neighborhood was full of families with children of similar ages to my siblings and me. During any free time that I was allowed (or could create by completing a chore quickly), I learned to play sports. Neighborhood pickup games occurred daily. Whiffle ball, football, baseball, basketball, hockey (when it was in season), and soccer were the main activities. Unfortunately, I did not have my dad's support to participate in formal sports, so I had to play during his workday or during what little time I could steal away from being his helper. As an example of his lack of support, when I did become involved with Little League baseball, he would never attend any games.

In later years he would not attend other sporting events in which I was involved, such as football games or wrestling matches. He told me once that I only participated in sports to be unavailable to work so hard with him. He maintained that attitude throughout my school years. It was a very selfish attitude, to say the least. I still needed to be a kid!

Near our house was a set of Rock Island Railway tracks with some fabulous bridges. My neighborhood friends and I would use them as our personal jungle gym when we could sneak away from our parents' sight. Those old wooden trestles across the Raccoon River and Walnut Creek were amazing places to spend a summer's day trying not to get hurt while doing acrobatic stunts. Trains traveled along the tracks often, from long and heavy freight cars to the fast-moving passenger cars. We would time our excursions to race the trains across the top of the trestle without falling or having to jump into the waters below. I know that is not in the standards of today's acceptable activities. I am not going to say we were the smartest about the potential dangers of those actions, but by some miracle, none of us were ever injured. The river was another place we played, and something we tried to keep hidden from our parents. What they did not know did not result in welts on our backsides.

There was always someplace to play in the neighborhood, and always someone's family watching out over the children. Even though we lived within the city limits, there were many small family farms nearby, and we would lightly harass the livestock in residence. One such family, the Cranovich clan, lived across the street from our house and kept a couple of dairy cows with an old bull in their large back acreage.

My friends and I would run around their pasture and fire up the bull as we practiced our version of Pamplona's running of the bulls festivities. We had a lot of fun, and no harm ever came to an animal. No children were hurt either, unless you include the time when old man Cranovich complained to my dad about what we neighborhood boys were doing. Dad severely compromised my ability to sit comfortably in school for a few days after one (and the last) incident.

The community operated as an extended family, and the neighbors all helped one another as best as the times allowed. This was a working-class area where families struggled to make ends meet most of the time. Many families grew their own food out of necessity. Most homes on our dead-end street had at least one acre of ground with expansive food gardens. (Larger houses were very small farms.) Some neighbors had apple orchards, and we spent many hours harvesting apples in the summer and fall. Some gnarly old cherry trees in other yards were harvested every July. The neighbors all put their extra produce and fruit on tables along the street for anyone to take during normal harvest periods.

My family grew tomatoes by the bushels. There were several dozen massive plants in our garden area that my sisters and I were responsible for weeding and harvesting. Mom and the girls could only can so many mason jars for our yearly needs, so the rest of the tomatoes were available for others to take if they wanted. I remember many harvests where we would put out two or three bushels daily and the neighbors would take them all.

I looked forward to attending school every fall. I admit I was often unruly in school; not because I was ornery or lacked discipline, but because I was simply very bored. It turns out I was very intelligent and far advanced for the grade I attended based on age. If my parents could have afforded the transportation to get me to a better-equipped school, I would have been enrolled in advanced placement classes. Those classes were not in the curriculum offered at my small neighborhood school. However, they could not find the funds. Because the local elementary school was within four blocks of our home, no transportation other than my own two feet was required. There was no busing for students in that era as is commonplace today.

I am fortunate to have had very understanding teachers assigned to my local elementary school who helped me navigate the early education system. During my elementary school years, my teachers would allow me to do advanced work away from the classroom and let me hang out in the school library. This was a common routine for me during large portions of the school days. The neighborhood elementary school was old with just a few classrooms in a three-story brick building that housed first through fourth grades. Built in the early 1920s, there were very few amenities and limited floor space. The gymnasium tripled as a classroom and an assembly hall. Two extra classrooms for students were in a small wing annexed to the original building.

The library was not much larger than a ten-by-ten-foot room and was located on the otherwise-vacant third floor next to an unused nurse's office. It had a single table, along with four walls full of shelves that stretched from floor to ceiling completely crammed with books. As small as it was, it was like a little bit of heaven to this young child's mind. The solitude I was afforded there was a welcome friend that allowed me to explore a world previously unknown. I was on my own to ramble through the novels, encyclopedias, and reference books.

I had to maintain perfect attendance and near-perfect grades to keep my library privileges, and I did not fail. I read often and voraciously throughout those days. I let myself dream of faraway vacation locales, exotic animals, alien life in the universe, and the pursuit of knowledge. This was where I developed my first (and only) principle I thought would lead to future success, which is having the ability to talk intelligently to any person about any subject at any time. Let us just say that I still consider this principle to be a work in progress.

We spent the better part of seven or eight years remodeling the house where I grew up. The house, built in 1903 by my dad's great-grandfather, had a lot of character. Not even the yard escaped our refurbishing efforts. We built patios, raised garages, dismantled old outbuildings and barns, and installed cement driveways. We added heating, electrical service, and running water to a converted shed that served as a dog kennel and built a garden and orchard.

Inside the house, we tore out old lathe plaster walls and installed paneling or drywall in the two-story home. We updated our coal furnace to a gas-forced air system, completely rewired the electrical system from the ancient knob-and-tube wiring with screw-in fuses to breaker panels with encased wiring, and made major changes to the existing minimal plumbing. While the house had some modern plumbing installed when we purchased it in 1960, there was still a working well with a hand pump just outside our back door and an abandoned outhouse in the backyard.

There was always a project to start or complete. Every day. Every night. Every weekend. All year long. When no active project was underway, the work centered on preparing for the next project.

I worked alongside Dad as the other pair of hands he often needed to hold a board, measure for a cut, paint a wall, clean up sawdust, haul out trash, and put the tools away (always in the correct place, of course). One of my not-so-favorite chores was the game I called tool fetch. Dad's workshop was in the basement and the trips up and down the stairs to get yet another tool wore me out. Dad would take me on excursions to construction sites where we would scavenge any useable scrap pieces for our next project. You might say we were early pioneers in the recycling and repurposing movement that would go mainstream years later.

Dad's constant projects meant I was seldom free to just hang out with my friends and do normal kid things during the school year. I was fortunate to arrive home from school about an hour before Dad got home from work. That hour allowed me just enough time to complete any assigned homework. The rare occasions when I had no homework assignments to complete, I had a free hour to play unless my mother had a chore that needed my attention.

As a positive offshoot of this work and time conscription, I learned a plethora of trade skills. I also learned that I really hated working some of those trades, particularly cement work. Stone and brickwork ran a close second. I did not mind the electrical work and never became particularly adept at the plumbing work. I was quite small in stature—the more physically taxing the work, the less I enjoyed it. Screeding concrete was hard and heavy work for someone my size with my muscle capacity. I preferred the more complex work (like electrical), which did more to occupy my mind and maintain my interest. I learned early on that hard work would be required in life, but the trades were not where I wanted to spend my life.

There were many outings, such as reunions, that we enjoyed as a family during the summertime. We attended every family reunion, which is odd as I look back, considering Dad did not like his family all that well. There were weekend fishing or camping trips to nearby state parks and occasional visits from friends and family. We would vacation every few years at my grandmother's house on Cape Cod in Harwich Port, Massachusetts.

Mimi, as we children called her, had a large house on Main Street with a small pizza restaurant in her front yard. Oh my, the aroma of that place! I remember it still. The pizza shop recipes and restaurant (Snow's Pizza, for any old-time Cape Cod residents who may be reading this) would play a very important part later in my life.

Overall, I thought we had a good life. I did not know at the time that I was missing anything or any part of a different life. I also did not suspect that life could or should be any different. I only knew what expectations of me existed. Not conforming to my dad's (and sometimes my mom's) expectations could result in very undesirable consequences. My sisters and I quickly learned to avoid negative attention at all costs.

Children only know about the world immediately around them: the cocoon their parents create, the neighborhood they grow up in, the school they attend, and the friends they make. I certainly did not have a reference point for comparison. I can guarantee you that nobody spoke of family issues or dysfunction outside of their immediate family in those generational times. To paraphrase what would become Vegas's marketing slogan fifty years later was how every household operated in that era: what happened at home, stayed at home. Nobody ever dared to air any family secrets in public.

There were issues that arose occasionally, but as children, we were only vaguely aware of the seriousness of them. Most days we just did our best to do our work and handle all our chores—rinse and repeat as necessary. Everyone in the neighborhood had the same goal: just live well and survive.

CHAPTER 2

My Preteen and Early Teen Years

I met Bill Yeager in middle school, and he was my very best friend for many years to come. Our meeting was the beginning of my exposure outside the small neighborhood clique I knew so well. Bill and I were inseparable in many ways, and he helped me see the world from a new and different perspective. Maybe it was the times (mid to late 60s) or our ages (ten to fifteen years old), but it was a magical time for me, and my new best friend made it so much better. School remained very easy for me, and I stayed on the honor roll as it afforded me extra privileges during school hours.

I started noticing girls as another gender instead of just other kids in the neighborhood or at school. A couple of them caught my eye in a major way. I will not name them to save any possible embarrassment for them (more so for myself) should they ever read this. To this day, thinking of them stirs up fond memories for me as I recall their smiles. In retrospect, I realize I was far too shy around girls during those formative years. I might still be too shy to some extent. I saw one of those special girls at our forty-year high school reunion and still felt flustered speaking to her.

My small stature presented many challenges the older I became. I was very short with a slight frame well into my very late teens. I was not Little Person small but was always at the lower end of any expected growth level. To give you some perspective, as a first-year student in high school, I had reached a height of four feet seven inches and weighed a whopping eighty-four pounds.

It was obvious I would never be a basketball star with that height, so I concentrated on baseball and football. Even football was a challenge because of my size. I may have been talented physically, but seldom was I selected when it came time to choose sport teams. Yes, I was that kid chosen last or almost last. I was just too small for people—even for my friends—to believe I was capable in most any sport. My advantage was brains over brawn, to be sure. It was always my mission to prove them wrong about my athleticism and, in my own mind, I did.

It was between elementary and middle school when Dad decided to open the West Des Moines Bait and Tackle store near our house. As a longtime resident and outdoorsman in the area, Dad was able to provide novice fishermen with bait along with some guidance about where to find the good spots along the Raccoon River or the area ponds where friendly farmers allowed strangers to cast their lines. The old-timers and Dad's many friends used the store as a hangout to drink beer and catch up on the latest news. The bait store was the nostalgic type that you see in the movies today—rustic, noisy from the air pumps in the live wells, and aromatic from baits and fish supplies. Hints of old cigarettes and cigars mixed with the smell of smoke from the small potbelly stove that took the chill out of the cooler mornings and evenings hung in the air. Looking back, it seems like a dream.

The store was open during the evenings and on weekends and kept us very busy once we completed remodeling the house. Dad owned and managed the bait shop while continuing to maintain his full-time day job. For me, there was little difference in my available free time—the store was just another project for his Boy Friday.

When I wasn't working evenings at the bait and tackle store listening to tales about the ones that got away from the fishermen clientele who hung out there, I was out obtaining live merchandise to stock the store. Weekday evenings after it had gotten dark outside, I (and often my sisters) would spend time in a local city park under the supervision of Mom or Dad. Armed with a flashlight and bucket, we would hunt for night crawlers on our hands and knees for hours. Rainy nights were always best for catching the worms.

Dad and I would wade through local creeks on weekends seining for minnows and crawdads or cane pole fishing for chubs. There were also times we would manufacture bait. Have you ever used cornmeal, chicken entrails, and a blender to make catfish bait? I have, and I can assure you it is as disgusting and smelly as one would surmise.

Spring, summer, and fall were very busy for the couple of years the bait store was open. Hard work keeping one's idle hands busy is good for you, Dad told me quite often. My lesson learned during this time was that you did whatever was needed to support the family. Questioning why you could not go out to play instead of working came at a price that I quickly learned was not worth paying.

CHAPTER 3

When Ignorance and Intolerance Came Calling

My older sister Kerry began having some problems that really ramped up the tension at home in the late sixties shortly after she became a teenager. There was a lot of arguing between her and our parents. I also seemed to be in trouble, even though I had done nothing to warrant inclusion. My dad always held the idea that, as the older (and only) brother, I needed to take care of my sisters and ensure they did nothing wrong. For the longest time, I had no idea why Kerry was in trouble. I only knew that I was also in trouble because Kerry was not behaving the way our parents expected her to behave and they seemed to think it was quite serious.

Even though Kerry did not want to talk to me about whatever she was experiencing, I eventually found out she was experimenting with an alternative lifestyle, and that was the genesis of the increased tension at home. Once I was aware of what was causing the family discord and strife, I totally understood her unwillingness to talk to me about her personal adolescent coming of age.

In retrospect, I realize I was much too young to help her with—or truly even fathom—whatever she was feeling about being gay if she had chosen to speak to me about it. Even from my insider's perspective, this was my first encounter with the world of sexual orientation, and I was just as bewildered and confused as she seemed to be. These things did not happen in our cocoon. My own naiveté was certainly on full display. I know now that I could have done more by simply just being there for her—whatever she needed. As it was, she stood mostly alone, and it saddens me to think how lonely that must have been for her.

When Kerry was sixteen years old, the altercations came to the tipping point. She had signed up to play softball in the West Des Moines Parks girls' league just as she had the previous few years. Mom and Dad had determined that the softball league apparently was where she had met the girlfriend who, in my parents' view, had "turned her." Mom and Dad blew a gasket about her situation and immediately removed her from the league. They were convinced that her choices were only environmental. More directly, they believed her inclination toward being gay was a result of the company of one girlfriend she kept.

In the strict, old-fashioned family traditions of our house, there was no way anyone could be gay. It was neither to be permissible nor tolerated. Mom and Dad decided she had to get away from *those* influences at school and in sports. In a quick and decisive manner, they chose to send her away. Kerry traveled by train to Cape Cod to live with Mimi and get her life *straight*ened out.

From the time we other children were informed Kerry would go to Cape Cod to the time it happened was less than one hour. Mom and Dad provided no reasons to us other children for her going to Massachusetts to live with Mimi. There was never an explanation provided to us for any decision made in our house. Dad had complete and absolute authority. Nobody dared question his decisions in any fashion. There was lots of shouting, a fair amount of crying from my mom and sisters, and a lot of bewilderment on my part. It was all just too crazy and happening far too fast for me to understand. We eventually learned that Mom and Dad did not want her "disease" to infect us other children, which provided their incentive to relocate her quickly.

In the few the moments we could steal to speak with one another before she left, Kerry told me that Dad was not her dad. *What?* There was no time for any explanation as Dad interrupted our conversation by walking into the room. Kerry left our home immediately. I did not see her or hear from her again for almost two years.

Kerry was eighteen when she decided to leave Cape Cod, return to Des Moines, and begin living on her own. Because she was not living at our family house, our contact was sparse, but she never spoke again of our earlier conversation. I always suspected her avoidance of the subject was due to the distinct possibility of severe ramifications from our parents if the secret of her parenthood got around to any of us other children. I had no idea her parental news included me until many years later.

I discovered several years after her return that Kerry had sent letters home during her stay with Mimi. Mom never shared those letters with me or my other two sisters. I also discovered that our parents had never mailed any of the letters we children wrote to Kerry. They determined it was best to shield Kerry from everything in Iowa to help keep her from being homesick. I imagine she must have felt a sense of abandonment when she did not receive any return letters from us.

I will never know for sure, however, as she passed away in February 2002. I can only look back and wonder if I could have done something different to make her understand how much her sisters and I missed her.

CHAPTER 4

Our Family Business Forms

While Kerry was away living in Cape Cod, Mom and Dad decided to open a pizza restaurant using the family recipes from Mimi's very successful pizza restaurant. We began by refurbishing an old diner in Norwalk, Iowa, that had closed many years earlier.

Dad and I worked at putting a new façade on the building in our efforts to spruce the place up and make it presentable. I painted the entire outside of it a horrible red color, and then we then set about working on the interior. We left the original dining area intact for the ambience of years past. The place had a lunch counter with a half dozen stools that would serve as the waiting area for our customers. The red coloring on the Formica counter showed extensive wear from years of patrons eating quick meals served with little fanfare.

We gutted and remodeled the preparation areas. We removed the grills and cooking ovens to install a massive pizza oven, and we overran the storage room in the back with newly installed refrigeration coolers. All available storage in the other small back room was crammed with utensils of the trade, including a large Hobart mixer for making dough and grating cheese. There was very little room for dry or canned ingredient storage, which necessitated multiple visits to the supply store each week. Supply delivery was available at a cost my parents would not pay. I became the supply runner any time I was not in school and ingredients were needed to replenish the stock.

We opened Connie's Pizza in 1972. The place was a true relic of the old days. The diner did not have even a single restroom for staff, let alone patrons. We relied on the facilities at the gas station next door, which was a short walk across the side driveway. That was very inconvenient, I must say. The diner cost next to nothing to purchase, and we carried a lease on the land. I think the great vision for Dad at the time was to refurbish the place and sell it once the business was established. He called it selling blue sky.

The building would never be worth much without restroom facilities, but there was always someone willing to buy the business. Dad certainly would not have provided them the recipes that have been in our family for decades, but he would sell them the customer base we had built up. It would be the responsibility of the new owner to keep those customers happy and coming back.

My younger sisters, Janelle and Brenda, worked there with me on every shift. During the day, Mom would do most of the prep work. She would handle the supply ordering, put sauces together, and make the dough. We children would work the evenings making pizzas and hot sandwiches. Mom was also responsible for cleaning the restaurant during the weekdays when school was in session and for picking up the supplies whenever I was not available. Janelle and I handled the preparation and cleaning work when we were not in school.

During exceptionally busy times, Mom and Dad would work along with us; however, (and I believe I can speak for Janelle as well as myself in this thought) they just got in the way. My sisters and I had developed our own refined system to keep up with the order volume and keep those pizzas moving out the door. Janelle and I made and filled the orders while Brenda handled the checkout and took the phone and walk-in orders. The operation was smooth—at least to us teenage kids.

Dad still maintained his full-time job and left it up to the rest of us to manage the pizza business. We were open for dinner from five o'clock to ten o'clock on weeknights and a bit later Friday and Saturday. We never opened for lunch hours, although there were lunchtime catering jobs during summer periods for special occasions as demand grew.

It seemed to Janelle and me that we pretty much ran the pizza place throughout our high school years. Brenda was young and very small, but she worked right along with us. Mom and Dad handled the books. Everyone worked hard because that was the mission: to succeed or fail as a family. Janelle would take on the brunt of the weekday daily work after I left for college a few years into the business. To this day, I can still make a killer pizza, although Janelle can probably outdo me in that realm. Even today, pizza making continues to be a family legacy, as we have passed on the recipes to our children, nieces, and nephews, who are keeping the tradition alive.

Eventually, we closed the pizza shop in Norwalk and moved the business to a new location on the south side of Des Moines. The building was a remodeled house with a masonry stone facade, so we changed the name of the business to The Stonehouse Pizza and Lounge. The decision to move the business happened after Janelle had finished high school and I had left for the military.

CHAPTER 5

My High School Years

During high school, schoolwork remained very easy for me. Because of my proficiency in my normal classes, I never really learned how to study properly, which would prove to be problematic in my later education efforts. I was fortunate (I guess?) that my academic abilities eliminated my need to study most of the time because my responsibilities to the family business began shortly after school was dismissed for the day, and they encompassed the entirety of my weekends. I am not sure when I would have found time for any additional schoolwork, otherwise. In the sparse time I had between school and the pizza parlor, I engaged in organized sports—much to my father's dismay and disapproval.

As has already been established, I was too short for basketball. I was also not a good enough swimmer for an accomplished swim team, so when baseball was out of season, wrestling was one of my sports of choice. It was Iowa, after all, and it seemed to be a state obligation. I joined the wrestling team and competed in the lowest weight class: ninety-eight pounds. The good news for me was that I never had to worry about making weight anytime I stepped on the scales before matches. I was good at wrestling and would have continued throughout high school had it not been for an elbow injury and my continued interest in girls.

I could not find time to handle my home chores, schoolwork, desire to chase girls, and wrestling. Something had to give, and that something was grappling. I had a little more luck with scheduling time to play on the baseball team in the spring and summer months.

Practices and games occurred earlier in the day during my free time. The activity did not interfere with my work hours at the pizza shop. Unfortunately, my size worked against me in the baseball coach's eyes, and even though I was truly good at my position as a catcher, I was only allowed to play for a couple of years before being given the opportunity to ride the pine to reduce the risk of injury.

While my size had been an asset to my wrestling endeavors, it led to my eventual elimination from the baseball and football teams. I was a very rugged kid who could play most sports well. The coaching staff did not clear me to play football due to the likelihood of injury after my first year. In their minds, a less-than-hundred-pound youngster attempting to tackle someone twice his size and weight only had one likely outcome, and it was not a good one. Even though I held my own as a defensive back or receiver in our local neighborhood games, the coaches deemed I could not stand the rigors of the organized game. I was certainly not afraid to block or tackle, just as I was not afraid to get hit or tackled by an opponent. It was everyone else who was afraid that I would get hurt—not me.

Looking back, I understand that the coaches were only looking out for what they thought were my best interests. At the time, though, I was very unhappy with their decision. To be honest, it was embarrassing in my mind. It made me feel like a lot less of a young man to be thwarted from engaging in what I viewed as a manly sport.

Size was also a huge detriment to dating during high school. I would ask a girl out for a date, and typically, I would be rejected with, "Oh, you're so cute," or something similar. Really? Cute? I did not want to be cute ... I was looking for the girlfriend experience (*wink, wink*). I was interested in spending free time away from home or school with some of the girls I thought hung the moon. I went out to too many parties as a crowd participant and always had a good time, but one-on-one dating was just not in the cards for me. I enjoyed the few dating experiences I had even though the dates were very rare. I was a friend to everyone but was never a boyfriend. I had to take solace in being cute.

It was during these high school years when the gilding began falling off the rose of what I thought was a good family life outside of the issues Kerry was having. I began learning there were serious issues between Dad and other members of the Vermeulen family, especially his father and his brother Clayton. As children, my sisters and I did not understand (and were never given) the reasons for the family dysfunction. All we knew or felt was the stress and tension in the air during any family gathering. As a result, our lesson learned was to be very tight among our own family of six. There was always an us-against-them atmosphere and expectation.

As an example of the family strife that occurred during the years leading up to and including high school, we could not visit my dad's parents even though they lived only eight short blocks from our family home. I would learn many years later of a family rift from Dad's younger years that was never resolved.

The woman I knew as Grandma Vermeulen passed away when I had just turned fourteen. We had lived within a few blocks of them for twelve years, and I do not recall seeing her more than three or four times at their house before we said our final goodbyes to her. Grandpa Vermeulen was around our home a bit more often after Grandma passed, but there was always a tenseness in the air during the visits.

CHAPTER 6

My First Taste of Real Freedom

High school went by in a flash, and it was away to college for me after graduation in 1974. I think high school had gone by so fast because all I did was go to school and then go to work. There was very little of anything else. Each of us children had a part in the family's success, and I felt especially responsible (valid or not). The pressures of being the only boy were immense for me. My dad held me to a different standard, regardless of subject. Disappointing him generally meant a very bad time for me. You learn to adapt and make sure there is nothing you fail.

I was off to Iowa State University and the freedom to make my own choices. I soon realized I was not ready for that freedom. I had never learned how to make good decisions, outside of avoiding my parents' negative attention. Fear of failure and the consequences from my dad that a failure would bring influenced my personal decisions throughout my early years. The knowledge that Dad would expect me to justify my choices based upon his scale of truth and acceptance was inhibiting. I had to face him every day and answer to whatever he might know or perceive during my life up to that point. Now I was on my own during the weekdays, having to answer to no one. I was out of control, reveling in the freedom that I had never known and never learned how to manage.

My choices were seldom good—drinking, carousing, and feeling I was too cool for school, so to speak. This was the mid-1970s, and I was full-on living the party life. The drinking age in Iowa was eighteen years of age at the time and I took full advantage of my new adult status. Thanks to the gift of my mind, school was still easy for me, although I was horrible at the process of college. My inability to study properly was a catalyst to my avoidance of class assignments, and I seldom actually attended classes. I was able to pass a few tests without much effort, but I did not really want the burden of attending classes, as it cut into my recovery time from the hangover that resulted from the previous night's partying. I was carrying a twenty-one-credit load in Electrical Engineering, and it was not enough. I was just not happy. Honestly, I felt the same way I had during elementary, middle, and high school. I was bored—seriously bored.

I would infrequently attend classes Monday through Friday. Whether I attended or not (usually not), I needed to keep the allusion of attendance alive for my parents. As soon as my last class ended on Friday morning, I would pack up what I needed for the weekend and drive back to Des Moines to work at Connie's Pizza. It was my job to pick up supplies on Friday afternoon, open the shop, and make pizza Friday night. On Saturday, we cleaned the restaurant in the morning, opened the shop mid-afternoon, and made pizza and sandwiches until restaurant closing. Sunday was a repeat of Saturday plus prepping for the Sunday evening shop opening before driving back to school following our Sunday afternoon family dinner. After the forty-five-minute drive back to college, I spent Sunday evenings doing my laundry in the dormitory and trying to determine what classes I might (probably not) attend during the coming week. This routine repeated for months. Same road trip Friday. Same road trip Sunday. Same partying during the week.

I had no social life during this time because of my weekend workload. Even during my weekly partying, the social dating aspect was still missing. Most girls I met at college were busy with classes and studying during the week. Duh! However, I was never in town on weekends when they were available for dates. I was quickly reaching a level of burned out and bummed out.

Shortly after my dad's birthday in mid-February, I decided I was done with college. I was going to do something else. I had to start living what I presumed would be a normal life. I do not recollect what I thought a normal life would be; however, I knew I was going to have one. What I do remember is that I had no time for a dating life, and that had to change immediately.

I arrived home from college unexpectedly one day and sat my parents down to discuss my school and work situations. The disappointment on Dad's face was evident the very moment I told them I had withdrawn from Iowa State University. I made up some excuse that sounded reasonable, at least to me, to avoid having to explain my actual reasons to him. The look he gave me as my decision sank in is one I will never forget. I was supposed to be the first one in his entire family to graduate college. Some had attended, but none had finished.

Mom's expression was just blank. I would guess partly due to her fear of Dad's reaction because his temper could often overwhelm him. Mainly, I think it was because she realized they had put too much pressure on me to be the everything-successful child.

CHAPTER 7

Steven, We Need to Talk

A few days after withdrawing from college and dropping the surprise-I'm-home bomb on my parents, I started looking for work. This was early 1975, and while the US involvement in the Vietnam conflict had mostly ended, it was still an ongoing concern. I thought about that a lot during my drives around Des Moines to fill out employment applications.

The military was still actively recruiting young men, but college had afforded me some deferment protection from the draft. Now that I had left college, I feared receiving *the letter* from the local draft board. Although the actual draft was over, registering and obtaining a lottery number was still required. My draft number for 1973 was twenty-eight. If the US Selective Service reinstated the draft, that was the last draft lottery available for their selection process. I had no doubt I would be available for selection. I recall not being afraid of going to fight in a war, but I certainly did not want the draft to send me into the US Army. At the time, all I knew about the Army was what I saw portrayed in military movies, and that did not fit with my plans to enter the electronic or technological fields.

I figured the odds were not in my favor, so I decided to try to get ahead of the curve. I stopped by a local recruiting office and enlisted in the US Air Force. Active-duty USAF, not National Guard and not Reserves—regular USAF. I was not going to hide from the war by choosing an easy route to meet the Selective Service requirements or run to Canada as a conscientious objector as was being reported on many of the television news stations at the time. After completing all the paperwork with the ever-so-welcoming recruiter, I needed only to provide a copy of my birth certificate to complete my enlistment. Little did I know that this piece of documentation was going to be the start of a forty-two-year odyssey that would eventually lead me to the family I have today.

I went home and asked my parents where I had been born so I could send for a copy of my birth certificate. I explained that I had joined the Air Force to avoid selection for a draft into the Army, and I needed it to complete my enlistment. My dad was quite accepting of my decision. He was certainly not happy that I had decided to leave college; however, he was proud I had chosen the military route. He reminded me that I could go back to college after my enlistment using the GI Bill. The wry smile on his face I saw was a step toward earning back some of his pride in me I knew had been diminished with my decision to leave college. The look on my mother's face was far different, though. Her face filled with a look of absolute horror.

When I asked for the information about my birth certificate, my naiveté regarding how official records were stored and maintained was on full display. I assumed the only record of my birth would be at the hospital where I had been born, and the document would be readily available to me if I sent for it. Could all those old movies be so wrong? At the time, I only knew I had been born on Cape Cod. There had been mention of places we had lived during our years on the Cape, but I recalled no stories told about where specifically each of us had been born. Mom told me she already had a copy of all our birth certificates, and I did not need to send away for one. She then told me I had been born at the Cape Cod Hospital in Hyannis, Massachusetts.

I initially thought Mom's look of horror might have been because of the ongoing Vietnam Conflict. There was not a television or radio station that did not cover it daily. I was soon to realize, however, that I thought wrong. My seemingly innocent request for my birth certificate was about to force her to divulge a family secret that was going to be exceptionally uncomfortable for her and potentially explosive. She looked at me and said in a very serious tone of voice: "Steven, we need to talk."

Dad left the room and Mom fetched my birth certificate from wherever she kept her valuable paperwork hidden. Before she handed it to me, she told me that some things about my family were different than I knew. She said she had been afraid to tell me then, just as she had been afraid to tell me at any other time during my childhood. Then she said the words that still ring in my ears: "Moe is not your father. Your father is Melvin Lee Kreider. Everyone calls him Sonny. Sonny is also Kerry's father."

Wow! My mind was instantly reeling with confusion. Suddenly, so many things made much more sense to me. Kerry and I were not Dad's children. Almost immediately, my mind began putting situations and outcomes together from our childhood experiences. There was a rush of so many memories. Those memories had previously seemed odd for no apparent reason. No wonder Kerry and I seemed to be the children to get the brunt of blame and punishment the majority of the time. True to form for those who were not stepchildren, Janelle and Brenda often went blame-free.

I finally understood why I was smaller in stature than my cousins and other Vermeulen family members. I suddenly understood why some people stopped talking about family connections at reunions, weddings, and funerals when I walked into the room. I understood the sideways glances whenever I said anything about being a Vermeulen. I always thought I was not wanted or that I was a leper in some fashion, but I had simply misunderstood all the telltale signs throughout my childhood. This was the first of many times I realized how secretive and manipulative my family was in how our lives transpired. There have been many more occasions that a past secret would bubble to the surface and leave me wondering why—or for what possible reason—there had to be a secret at all.

The fallout of the fatherhood admission was immediate. The only dad I had ever known stopped speaking to me for several weeks. I was quite bewildered by his actions because it felt like I had done something wrong even though I knew I had not. It was a very long time before he and I spoke about that moment, but suffice to say, he thought I would reject him when I learned the truth about him and the man whose name was on my birth certificate.

Looking back to that time with the knowledge I now have about my dad's early life, I can understand why he might have had that concern. His father had rejected him during his early adulthood, and he was often on the receiving end of extremely harsh discipline as a child. This was a familiar circumstance for him. I think the most powerful words I could use came to me when I finally confronted him about his lack of interaction toward me. Those words changed our relationship for the better when I said to him: "It takes more to be a dad than it does a father." We maintained a strong bond until he passed in 2016, and I always continued to call him Dad.

CHAPTER 8

My Name Is What?

Suddenly armed with this new name, I was dumbfounded. My real name was not Steven James Vermeulen. It was Steven James Kreider. Except for my birth certificate, every record I had was in the name of Steven James Vermeulen: my school records, my medical and dental records, my driver's license, my recently issued Social Security number, my USAF enlistment, and my baptismal record (though I did not find that one out until *many years later*).

I cannot begin to tell you the crazy things that went through my young mind. *How do I change any of these documents? Am I still obligated to anything I agreed to as Vermeulen? Do I need to start school over?* I know that last idea seems particularly silly, but I have a vivid memory of that crazy thought. *What will the rest of the family think of Kerry and me? Who else, if anyone, in the family knows? Oh, my goodness! What awaits me as I begin life with a new name?*

As it turned out, I soon learned I did not have to worry about a name change; I just had to continue as Vermeulen and provide accurate information any time something relative to my birth name came up. To the USAF, I became Steven James Vermeulen nee Kreider.

I talked to Kerry about this new and unexpected information and how I finally understood her statement to me as she was being whisked away to go live with Mimi a few years earlier. She told me that she had been searching for Sonny Kreider, and while she had not found him, she intended to continue looking.

Moe did not adopt Kerry and me, and Mom further explained

why our names are Vermeulen regardless of our birth records. I learned then that there does not need to be a legal change to use a name other than what name is on your birth certificate. The only requirement is that you do not use a new name to commit any type of fraud. Once the fatherhood discussion occurred and we shared the family secret with Janelle and Brenda, Kerry changed her name back to Kreider from Vermeulen, and Kerry Lee Kreider was her official name for her remaining days.

Mom allowed me a few days to come to grips with the big news before beginning to explain to me how my situation had come about. Unfortunately, her explanations left me with many false and contradictory impressions about the happenings of those years during the 1950s and my father. Mom told me she had divorced Sonny because he had been seeing another woman by the name of Pat Wells. Pat had become pregnant with a son at the same time Mom was pregnant with me. During another discussion, she told me Sonny had left her when he found out she was pregnant with another child (me) because he did not want any more children.

Which version of her story was I to believe? The one where she kicked him out because of another woman being pregnant or the one where he left because Mom herself was pregnant with a child he did not want? If it was the former (which is the story my mother repeated many times over the years), then that meant I had a half-brother out there somewhere who had been born in the early spring of 1956 and was just a few months younger than me.

My mother's explanations continued to twist and turn over the next several years, and the stories did not always match cohesively. From the timeline I could put together, Kerry would have been no more than a few weeks old when Mom parted ways with Sonny the first time. Sonny supposedly did not take to fatherhood well and was not particularly capable of caring for the infant Kerry. Mom also told me that Sonny never wanted anything to do with me (*that* was certainly not at all helpful to my self-esteem) and had never seen me even once. Mom never really gave a reason for his refusal to see me, saying only that whenever she would contact him about visiting his children, Sonny would only agree to see Kerry. The essential point is that Mom always portrayed Sonny as a noncommittal womanizer.

I had no reason to question her version of events at the time.

Based on the outcome of more than a few of her stories, I have learned over the years that her characterizations were probably not entirely accurate. While Sonny may have been a cad about many things, there is no evidence to indicate he was anything more than a young and foolish man who was not yet ready for the responsibilities of a wife and children.

Dad had a horrible jealous streak that would surface often, especially if Mom ever dared to speak about her past husband. He viewed the discussions as if she had the intention of a personal betrayal toward him. The topic of Sonny, or even the mere mention of his name, always brought out an immediate anger. Unfortunately, he often became physical when angered, as we learned so well during our early years. That anger from Dad was something the family always tried to avoid. Due to the subject matter and previous experience, the conversations Mom and I had about Sonny or the alleged half-brother were always held without the knowledge or involvement of Dad.

Her stories always started with the assertion that the other woman—Pat Wells—had died when the boy was around two years old, and Sonny had supposedly raised him alone after her death. To her knowledge, Sonny and Pat had never married. Pat was from the same area of Delaware where Sonny had grown up and where the Kreider family had firmly planted roots. The situation and information were disturbing to me. Mom had made it clear that Sonny was not the fatherly type to Kerry and that I was not wanted by him at all ... yet, he had raised his younger son alone. I found this ironic, to say the least.

Many of the stories told to my sisters and I seem unbelievable in hindsight, but we just took them at face value because we had no reason to doubt our mother's story at the time. I also had no other resource (or reason, really) to confirm or validate her stories with someone else. I certainly could not ask Dad without stirring up his anger, and most of my mother's family who might have knowledge of this era had passed away by the time Mom relented and provided any information. With the sparse information I had about Pat Wells and my father, I began searching for both my birth father and my half-brother.

CHAPTER 9

My Search Begins

In the time before the internet was realistically commercially available, my progress was slow. I was unable to find any confirming information for nearly fifteen years. Kerry had been doing her own research and had learned our father was living in Florida. She never explained how she determined his location, however, I suspect she may have obtained some clues to his whereabouts during her two-year stay with Mimi.

Curiously, Kerry never mentioned trying to find our half-brother. In fact, she seemed completely unaware of that part of our mother's story. I probably should have gotten a hint about the viability of my information at that time, but it simply did not occur to me that Mom was telling Kerry one story and telling me a different one.

Kerry eventually caught up with Sonny via phone and, by all accounts, it was not a positive experience for her. She told him about her alternative lifestyle early into her first call, and that ended their conversation abruptly before she was able to broach the subject of me with him. As Kerry was explaining the details of her contact to me, I could sense her deep sadness at the rejection by a third parental figure; it was quite evident in her facial expressions and her tears. She had always looked upon the non-acceptance of her lifestyle by Mom and Dad as a personal slight, and this was yet another burden for her to carry and one more disappointment to bear.

After her debacle with Sonny, Kerry shared with me the information she had been able to gather about our father. He resided in the Tampa, Florida, area from the late eighties through the early nineties and worked as a building general contractor. I would later learn that he had used his skills as an expert artisan in cabinet making to start his own home building business. With his contact information in hand, I attempted to reach out to Sonny multiple times over the course of three or four years. He never answered his personal phone or responded to any of the messages I left on his answering machine, which seemed odd for a man running a business.

When I was finally able to reach him, my experience was also negative. Our short call culminated with him asking me if I was queer too. I ended the conversation quickly; there was nothing more to say between us at that point. I was only interested in learning about some family history and did not need him nor his prejudices in my life.

Out of respect for Kerry, I only spoke with him one more time when I called to let him know that she had passed away. That was nothing more than a two-sentence conversation. It is sad how some people treat their family. I vowed to continue trying to find my half-brother even though Sonny was no longer a resource for information. I would need to move forward in the search.

Over the next few years, I spent a great deal of time searching the internet for any clue to Pat Wells with hopes she would be the key to finding my half-brother. As the internet grew and a many more records became public, I repeated the searches from time to time, hoping for a new lead. Never did a new lead pan out. Information on the internet continued to grow daily as local and state governments, businesses, and industries digitized their records. I never did obtain a solid hit.

Newspapers became another great source of content as publishers made their information available via the internet. I was quite thankful for the digitizing efforts. The availability of so much online content eliminated a lot of the library time previously needed to peruse hours of microfiche archives.

Even though I was able to rerun searches quickly using the same criteria every few years via the internet, information specific to my half-brother was still nearly impossible to find. Eventually, I began using the search tools on a DNA testing service site that has amassed a wide array of reference libraries within the past ten years.

With only general criteria from my knowledge of Pat Wells, the DNA services company records search provided me with more than fifty thousand possibilities for a Pat, Patty, Patricia, or P. Wells from Delaware. Without a formal name or date of birth, I knew it would take many years to research that exhaustive list.

I decided to try another avenue that I hoped might have better and more focused results. I searched the online newspapers for any matching obituary and was rewarded with a total of zero matches using very specific dates and names. At first, I focused on obituaries in Massachusetts and Delaware. Slowly, I expanded my search area to the northeastern states, but each state I added resulted in no matches. When I look back at the search information with a critical eye, I did not even know if any of my criteria were correct. According to my mother, Pat had died when her son was just two years old. I presumed that Pat would have been somewhere near my mother's age and placed her birth year between 1934 and 1938. As the child was born in 1956, that meant I was looking for a death in 1958 or 1959.

I did find there are many Pats who were resting in peace. I could not find one that had the lifespan I was surmising. Because some states have no public records available online, this was as much as I could accomplish without making a trip to a county registrar's office in a state I could only guess was correct and manually reviewing records.

I tried to find any marriage or birth records in the state of Delaware for Pat and still came up with no results that were even remotely close. I chose Delaware because Massachusetts records were not available online at the time for most counties. I thought maybe I would get lucky and find a marriage to someone else in her hometown area. After all, just because she did not marry Sonny did not mean she could not have married another man. Dead end. Then I thought perhaps I could find something related to her birth record that would point me toward another member of her family who could be a resource for information about her life, but again, without a proper name and location, I ran into another dead end. Every possible way I searched for Pat Wells led me nowhere.

When I could not find any credible information for Pat, I decided to change my focus to trying to find the child. I asked Mom what she recalled about the birth time or date, and all she could share was that the son was born in the hospital located on Otis Air Force Base in the spring of 1956. Being born on the Air Force base instead of in the local hospital meant there would be no state or local birth registry entry, or so I believed. This was particularly problematic because the base hospital had closed more than fifty years earlier. The information would be federal record data, and I had no idea where to begin a search that would allow me access to those birth records.

I presumed I could go through the process of applying with the Federal Freedom of Information Act to get the records; however, I needed to have specific and credible data on which to base the search. I was also sure I would need to find out where the records were stored before I started researching into how to start the process. I did not know if military birth records would be classified information or available to the public. I did not think a general letter to the Pentagon saying I wanted a list of all children born in early 1956 at Otis AFB would beget a review or reply and decided I would save that avenue for another time.

The countless hours I spent trying to locate any information relating to Pat Wells or my half-brother were frustrating. I wanted to give up many times and just let my known world keep revolving, but I just could not let it go. Some thing or some instance would remind me that I was missing a brother, and I would go back into the search with renewed hope. I would occasionally ferret out a promising lead only to hit a brick wall midway through the subsequent search. I spoke with many an understanding person as I explained my story and eliminated their families as leads. I was able to give pointers and encouraging support to folks who were also doing their own searches for relatives who crisscrossed with my research.

I was amazed at the number of people who were looking for lost members of their families when stories from years past were uncovered. Every part of my search was a learning and sharing experience even though the results were empty. I hope those whom I may have helped along the way ended up with far more positive results than I had obtained in my efforts to find my half-brother.

CHAPTER 10

A Father and Family Are Found

In 1994, I used some very general search criteria in conjunction with phone directory assistance and found an uncle from the Kreider side (Uncle Miles) in Wilmington, Delaware. While speaking with Uncle Miles—and kudos to him for being kind, patient, and generous with his time—I found out Sonny was pretty much a loner and had mostly been rather secretive about his life. Uncle Miles did not know anything about Sonny having a son near my age. He did not know about me, for that matter, and had only limited knowledge of Kerry (whom he had lost track of many years earlier).

Uncle Miles informed me that my grandmother, Bertha Kreider, was living in Wilmington, North Carolina, with her daughter, Shirley, and son-in-law, Raeford. He suggested I contact them for more information. Grandma and Grandpa Kreider had moved to Wilmington, North Carolina, so they could to be closer to family as they aged after their retirement. I thought my luck was turning with that contact because I was living in Raleigh, North Carolina, at the time, and Grandma Kreider was a mere two-hour drive away. I could easily coordinate with Aunt Shirley to plan meetings with a few of my Kreider relatives and get some answers that would aid me in the search for my half-brother.

Grandma Kreider was in her early nineties and in failing health by the time we met. She asked about Kerry and wanted to know how I had been. While the conversation was pleasant, Grandma Kreider suffered from dementia and was not able to recall much from her earlier life. Most of the conversations I had during each visit were with Shirley and Raeford. When I asked about my half-brother, Aunt Shirley was always evasive and only stated that she and her longtime military husband, Raeford, had been overseas during that time and she knew nothing about him or his mother. Grandma Kreider did not recall another grandson; she only had memories of Kerry. I do not recall catching the fact that she did not remember me because my attention was focused on the family history and my half-brother. The story of how Sonny was secretive in his life and did not share much with the family repeated often. *What is it with all the secrets that surround me in my family?*

I saw Aunt Shirley and Grandma a couple of times each of the next few years; however, they were not very good at keeping in touch with me. When Aunt Shirley's husband, Raeford, passed away, they did not call. Grandma Kreider passed away in October 2002, and I did not find out until two months later when I called to arrange a holiday visit.

CHAPTER 11

I Think I Found My Brother

       ood communication was clearly not a Kreider family trait. In the spring of 2007, I got word during a call with Aunt Shirley that Sonny had passed away in the fall of 2006. He had been living in Sevierville, Tennessee, which was about a five-hour drive from my home. I tracked down his obituary from the local newspaper as soon as I could get to a computer. I hoped it would be the break I needed to help me find my elusive half-brother.

    The obituary provided the name of Melvin L. Kreider Jr. from Kodiak, Tennessee. *Finally, a name!* With this solid lead and the internet as a strong partner, I was able to track down a phone number for Mel Jr. He proved to be just as tough to reach as Sonny had been. When I was finally able to contact him, it was first through his wife. After I explained my story to her, she readily facilitated a call between Mel Jr. and me.

    I made phone calls on multiple occasions over the following two-year span and received plenty of cautious suspicion from his side. Mel Jr. had no knowledge of me prior to my first phone call with him. He had heard rumors about Kerry, but had never had any personal contact with her. He also indicated he had never had any conversations with Sonny about other siblings; he had just assumed he was an only child for his entire life.

    When I was finally able to convince Mel Jr. that I had no ulterior motives such as claiming any inheritance or birthright, we decided I would drive to Kodiak, Tennessee, so we could meet and chat face-to-face. Finally, in 2014, I was going to meet my half-brother after a long, long search.

I remember being very excited on the drive across Interstate 40 toward Tennessee that my search of many years was finally at an end. Unfortunately, the meeting was rather anticlimactic. My first impression upon meeting him was that we were not similar in any way. Whereas I had high expectations and desires concerning the future of our relationship, his nervousness and suspicions were still front and center.

We had no physical characteristics in common that I could see. At a height of five nine, I was seven or eight inches taller and at least seventy pounds heavier than he was. Perhaps it was due to us having different mothers, but you would think some similarity of some sort would exist. Our only commonality was that neither of us had any sign of male-pattern baldness. I noticed that he did have some traits in common with Kerry, such as in height and coloration.

Upon meeting Mel Jr., I was able to gather more facts for comparison with the information given to me by my mother and found many things that did not align. Mom told me my half-brother would be a few months younger, but Mel Jr. is nine years younger. Mom said the mother's name was Pat Wells, but his mother's name is Elizabeth. Coincidentally, as Mom had said, Mel Jr.'s mother did pass away when he was two years old. I had to conclude that he was not the half-brother I was looking for but a different half-brother I had not previously known about.

Since that meeting with Mel Jr., I have completely lost track of him, and he has not attempted contact with me even though our meeting had been pleasant and cordial. Maybe he knew more about me than he acknowledged during our many hours of phone calls. Perhaps, with any curiosity he may have had satisfied, he could see no reason to maintain any further relationship with me.

He can still reach out to me if he ever feels the need, as he is a half-brother in my family. He has almost no electronic footprint and seems to prefer living mostly off the grid. His communication seems to be on par with that of other members of the Kreider family.

CHAPTER 12

Spitting in a Tube

During the past few years, I have seen various television shows about finding family and lost relatives. Most make me teary-eyed and hopeful that all works out for the families portrayed. I presume the emotion comes from my extensive search for a lost brother that had achieved no results. *Long Lost Family* on A&E is one such show. A DNA testing service is the primary sponsor and uses the show for heavy exposure via commercialization. I had joined that specific service several years earlier to take advantage of their family tree building tools during the search for my half-brother. The show gave me renewed hope that I could find the success, and ultimate happiness, generally portrayed by the stories.

I had nearly run out of leads from this electronic source and usually gotten the same secretive loner storyline about Sonny and his family activities whenever a new lead would produce a link to another Kreider family member. Watching one of the show's episodes in January 2017 struck a mental chord with me and pushed me to renew my efforts to find my half-brother. It was near the date of my birthday, and I was feeling the loss of Kerry, as our birthdays were within two calendar weeks of one another. I thought about ordering their advertised DNA test.

It had dawned on me quite suddenly that it was entirely possible my alleged half-brother might also be looking for his relatives. How could I have overlooked that possibility before that moment? That was one factor in my decision to submit a sample for DNA testing. It was not just about my search and me; I could be thwarting someone else's dream of finding me or other family members.

I talked to Melody about the possibility of using this avenue to search for my brother and she indicated it was a good idea. With her full support, I decided to order the DNA kit. It arrived in just a few days, and I returned the sample the next day. I was overly anxious to get the party started. The directions indicated a processing cycle of six to eight weeks, after which I could expect the results via email. I was hopeful that they would contain a clue and that I would be able to find the half-brother I had never met but had always known existed and wanted in my life.

When the DNA results arrived in my email a few weeks later, I could not have been more excited and anxious to explore the identified relatives. Among the initial number of 255 fourth cousin or closer DNA relatives in the database, I noted two individuals shown as my first cousins and four individuals listed as my second cousins. There were no relatives listed as half-siblings, however, and I lost a bit of my initial enthusiasm.

One family match, though, was very intriguing. The DNA results showed username *philw703* as a first cousin. I could think of no cousins with the first name of Phil or Philip, yet a first cousin would be someone very close to me and most likely a child of my parent's siblings. I thought I knew all my first cousins on my maternal side and concluded *philw703* would have to be a relative from my paternal side. To my knowledge, none of my paternal aunts and uncles had children named Philip. This might indicate I was getting closer to the half-brother, but I still could not piece that connection together.

I sent messages through the DNA services website to *philw703* and the other first cousin listed with username C.H. Within days, C.H. (through his wife, Reba) responded, and I learned that C.H.'s real name was Chris Holt. His surname was not surprising, as my mother's birth name is Holt. During our correspondence, we determined that Chris's father (Gaylord Holt) is my mother's half-brother. It turns out I was wrong in the assumption that I knew all my maternal first cousins because I was not aware of my mother's half-siblings. She had never spoken much about her father or extended family. He had been out of her life since she was only six years old. Imagine that ... At sixty-one years of age, I was learning about another branch on the Holt family tree.

After waiting a few days and not receiving a response from *philw703*, I sent a second message through the DNA service site. I waited a couple more weeks and sent a third. (As of the time of this writing, I have still never received a response to any of the queries I sent to *philw703*.)

How did *philw703* fit in as a first cousin? This user was going to be my key—I was sure of it. I could virtually eliminate him from my maternal side based on all the information I had gathered. After learning of my mother's half-brother, Gaylord, through my communications with Reba Holt, she referred me to Chris's sister, Candace, to get additional Holt family knowledge.

Through Candace, I learned that my mother had another half-brother named Jonathan who was alive and living in Texas. Candace was very gracious answering my questions and gave me the needed contact information for Jonathan, thinking I might obtain answers from him to questions she could not help with.

I called Jonathan and had a well-intentioned and pleasant conversation with him. He had no children named Phil or Philip, and his remembrances of the Holt family were minimal. He and his brother (Gaylord) had been adopted when they were very young, though they had retained their Holt surname. Unfortunately, he did not want to learn about or explore much of what I knew about the Holt family. He told me that ship had sailed for him. He had been emotionally hurt enough when he previously expressed interest in learning more about the Holt family history and had been rebuffed. For the most part, he had many proverbial doors closed in his face, and in his words, he was too old to care any longer. It was a sadly defeated attitude he carried.

Because we knew Chris Holt was from my maternal side and with still no answer from *philw703*, Melody and I tried to determine which of the listed second or third cousins I should contact next. There were three DNA matches listed as third cousins, two of whom were brothers. One of the brothers reached out to me well before I had a chance to send him an inquiry, so that decision became moot.

Because of the notification options I had selected on the DNA testing service when I released my results as public, close DNA matches (provided they also opted to publicly release their results) automatically received an email about new matches with me. The third cousin brothers and I chatted via email and by phone a couple of times and cemented our connection through the family of my maternal grandmother, Mimi.

The last of the six third cousin or closer family matches was a username P.R. As with C.H., that was not much to go on. Usernames with a strong hint of anonymity are very prevalent on the DNA service sites. I sent a hello message and asked for a response to help me determine our connection. I received no response for several months, after which we exchanged a few emails and phone calls. By the time we did connect, I had already determined the family relationship and knew she was related to me through the paternal lineage that I was trying to figure out during my initial contact.

It did not dawn on me until much later, when Melody pointed it out, that I did not have any listed relative matches with the surname of Kreider in my results. Hmmm ... That was an interesting twist.

I moved on to other avenues in my continuing quest to reach *philw703*. If he was not from my maternal side, that left only one option. He had to be from my father's side, and I had to be getting close to the half-brother Kreider. This would be so much easier if he would just respond to my messages!

How could he be a first cousin? Was he possibly a child given up for adoption by one of my aunts? My mother had two sisters, and Sonny Kreider had three. I suppose it was possible that one of my uncles had a child as well. Both parents had one brother, and none of their children were named Phil or Philip.

I was not aware there could be any other connection for a first cousin. Then I read the relationship designations on a DNA FAQ page and thought: *What the heck?* It turns out that DNA reported relationships on their sites are based on the number of steps two people were away from a common ancestor. The numerical designations, such as first cousin, could also be a niece, nephew, aunt, or uncle. Second cousins can be first cousins twice removed, etc.

The extended family naming convention remained confusing to me. So maybe *philw703* was not a first cousin; instead, maybe I had turned up a nephew or an uncle. This just added more confusion, and I began to consider purchasing an erasable whiteboard to keep it all straight as I moved family connections around. The tree was beginning to look like a spider web.

CHAPTER 13

Weeks?

Within a few days of my DNA results being publicly released on the testing service site, my second cousin, Theresa Olande, became (both literally and figuratively) the second cousin to contact me. She suggested we discuss our newfound DNA connection over a phone call. She explained that my name came up in her family relative matches, and she was quite eager to determine how I fit into her family tree. Theresa was on a mission to find her birth father and thought I would be a promising lead. We were able to rule me out as a lead in that search quickly because the father she is searching for is Filipino and I have no Asian ancestry.

While discussing how we could be DNA related, the only option from her perspective became a connection to her mother's side, and Theresa provided her mother's birth name as Weeks. I had several long phone conversations with Theresa over the next month as we tried to correlate all the information. I explained I had found no mention of Weeks anywhere in my family tree. I had run the trees back as far as the 1500s in some ancestral lines, and there was no Weeks found. I shared my tree with her on the DNA service site where she could research for herself and see if there were any other possible connections. I promised her I would continue researching my lineage and also ask my mother if she knew of any connections to the Weeks family.

I called my mother the day after my initial conversation with Theresa as I had promised. I told Mom I had done DNA testing to see if I could find my half-brother. I told her that my research was still not getting close to my intended target after all the years I had searched. I again confirmed the mother's name was Pat Wells and verified any other sparse information she could recall. I explained all the dead ends I was reaching as I researched the mother's name without more precise details. I asked if she knew of any Weeks in the family because a Weeks family descendant had contacted me after my DNA results were published. She said she did not know of anyone named Weeks. This was in May 2017. I am sure she did not really or fully understand the DNA science and that DNA match results are scientific fact and largely indisputable. DNA simply does not lie. She certainly did not realize that DNA results could identify close family relationships.

With Mom's dismissal of any known Weeks connection, I felt there had to be another explanation. I began thinking of any abstract possibilities that could logically explain the missing connection. Perhaps, if adoption had occurred for my half-brother because his mother had passed when he was young, his name was changed. I had already confirmed with Mel Jr. that there was no older brother raised by Sonny whom he knew, so adoption seemed like a reasonably valid theory. I began by considering ages and birthdays.

Because I am a grandfather, it is possible my half-brother could also be one and Theresa was a daughter or granddaughter of his. Theresa was fifty-seven at the time, and her mother was in her late seventies. I was sixty-one, so that timeline did not work for her to be that closely related. Further, Theresa's mother could not be an unknown sibling of mine and be that much older based on simple math given my father's birthdate. If her mother was a sibling of mine or had been in a relationship with my father, Theresa would rank closer than a second cousin. This seemed to be the wrong avenue; Theresa and I had to find our connection elsewhere.

Not knowing much about my paternal side resulted in unforeseen consequences. What other possibilities existed that could tie our DNA results together? I had no other living relatives on my mother's side I could reach out to for explanation or information. All relatives on my father's side were similarly gone or unreachable. Was Theresa wrong? I thought she must be DNA related via the Holt or Kreider sides somewhere and she was looking at the wrong connection or misinterpreting her results.

In my next conversation with Theresa, after speaking with my mother, I told her about my mother's dismissal of any known Weeks connection. We agreed there must be another link. Theresa further explained that she was working with another of her cousins (one not related to me) who was a genealogist, and she was certain we were DNA related on the Weeks side. I could find no definitive answer for our connection, and no hint of a clue existed. I promised Theresa I would continue to work at finding an answer from my side as she continued working from her side to fit the pieces together.

CHAPTER 14

I'm Getting Close

While I was working on one angle with Theresa chasing the Weeks link, I sent another message via the DNA testing service to *philw703* in hopes of getting a response. I was determined to find out what our familial relationship was. Another week passed with no answer. At this point, I was feeling stymied by the lack of options available to facilitate contact. With no response, were there any other options to find and identify the elusive *philw703*? I took to the mighty internet and threw what amounts to a Hail Mary pass.

I used an internet search engine to look for the username. Amazingly, I got a hit. *Philw703* had responded on social media to a food critic's review, and that gave me a small lead. I read the review and saw the name Philip Tyler was associated to the *philw703* remark. *Tyler? What? Dang it!* I was looking for a Weeks, not a Tyler. My initial thought was, *Crapola—another name to add to my family tree!* As with the name Weeks, I did not recall any Tyler in the research I had completed up to that point. The adoption thought crossed my mind again. *No silly, that would have shown as half-brother, not a first cousin.* It became clear that I was going to have to pursue more internet searching and reaching out to other testing services that identified DNA relatives in my quest to find answers. I really needed *philw703* to respond to my queries.

As I searched Philip Tyler's timeline on a social media site, I noted he had an open friend list I could peruse. His list included a few friends with the last name of Weeks: a Charles Weeks and a Chuckie

Weeks. That seemed interesting and provided me an opening to do some additional social media investigating. I had to determine if he was the connection I was chasing and rule out coincidence. It was far more promising than any other lead I had to research at the time, and it started my investigative juices flowing once again.

I read back through Philip Tyler's timeline and, fortunately, found a post from a couple of years earlier showing Philip had been the recipient of an Employee of the Month award. The posting had a picture of the award plaque. Congratulations! In big, bold lettering was the name *Philip Weeks*. Shazam! Light bulb moment! Philip Tyler was Philip Weeks. He must have been using his middle name of Tyler for some semblance of internet privacy.

I felt I had reached that *Eureka* moment, and I could not wait to explore more information regarding Philip Tyler Weeks. If I could only get him to respond. I was now certain *philw703* was my link to Weeks—I just did not know how that relationship fit into my known family tree.

I called my mother again on the morning of July 8, 2017 and updated her on where my research had taken me thus far. I needed to ask her a few additional questions, and I told her she had to help me understand why I was finding family ties named Weeks. I explained carefully that Philip Tyler Weeks is a first cousin of mine through DNA matching, but that I could not find any reference to anyone named Weeks in our family history. This was the second Weeks connection that was confirmed. I could not place either within the information I had found when I built my very extensive family tree. One might be a coincidence, but two pointed to fact. I simply needed her to answer more questions.

CHAPTER 15

Steven, We Need to Talk (Again)

I started by asking my mother some extremely tough questions and probing her for more family secrets. There were just too many things that were not matching up to any of the information I had been given. Was it possible there was an out of wedlock situation in the family? I knew Mimi had two sisters with no children of their own. Mom's answer was, "No, that did not happen." Okay. How about an adoption or some situation where a child from the Holt side ended up with a different name? Again, her answer was no.

Okay then, was it possible that she had the name wrong—that Pat Wells was maybe Pat Weeks, and I might be getting close to the half-brother's family name? That answer was also no. She explained that she had known Pat Wells personally, and her name was correct. All right then, something was just not making sense. If I was DNA related to the Weeks family, I could not find out through whom, yet DNA does not lie. Then she said those words again ... "Steven, we need to talk."

Oh great, I thought. *What now?*

That Saturday morning at around ten o'clock was when the truth came out. She began by telling me that my father was not Melvin Lee Kreider. *What?!* She continued by telling me I should not be so inquisitive because the knowledge she was about to give me could cause problems for other people. She called me a "real shit" for pursuing the Weeks connection and told me it was very embarrassing for her.

She then proceeded to tell me that my father is a man named Chuck Weeks from the Portsmouth, New Hampshire, area. She went on to explain that she had met him at Otis Air Force Base shortly after she had sent the philandering Sonny packing. She told me she had plans to marry Chuck, but it did not happen. She gave me no reason as to why the marriage did not happen. After a bit of what, what, and *what*, I thanked her for finally telling me the truth and began thinking about how I was going to re-channel my investigation with these new revelations. I needed to start trying to figure out who and where Chuck Weeks was. I now had an explanation of the Weeks connection, but how did it fit in with Philip and Theresa? My search had suddenly taken a completely new direction.

During her admission of my biological father's name, Mom took the time to explain her situation, including how I became a Kreider. She told me she had dated Chuck for a while after kicking Sonny out. (The time frame was probably not too relevant at that juncture of her explanation.) She admitted she had never told Chuck anything about me; she had never even told him she was pregnant. Sonny had come back into her life for a very brief period to give their marriage another shot, so she stopped seeing Chuck without any explanation to him.

The reconciliation with Sonny did not last long once Mom's pregnancy became evident. As the story goes, Sonny quickly realized he was not the father and left again for good. This was in stark contrast to one of her explanations years earlier that Sonny had left because she had become pregnant again so soon after Kerry's birth and he did not want another child.

She was still married to Sonny at the time of my birth even though he was gone from the marriage. Because of the state laws of Massachusetts at the time, the husband's name appeared on the birth certificate as the father regardless of who the biological father might be. She did not divorce Sonny until late 1956. Even though she filed for the divorce in May of that year when I was just a few months old, the cooling-off period required by Massachusetts state law was six months, and couples could give their marriage a do-over with no harm, no foul. Because Sonny was in the Air Force during that time, Mom was able to maintain full military spouse and family benefits because both Kerry and I are his children per our birth certificates.

Newly single, Mom resumed going to the Air Force base, using it as her primary dating venue. Along with her older sister, Faith, she visited Otis Air Force base many weekends to dance and have some fun. Her recollection of life during that period, while certainly faded by time and lost memories, was about taking care of her children while working at various serving jobs, as well as making pizza for Mimi's pizza restaurant. At the time, Snow's Pizza was still a carryout-only store. A weekend night out on the town while Kerry and I were watched by my mother's younger sister, Sandra, was her one weekly highlight.

Mom started dating Moe just after my first birthday. Young adults doing what young adults do, she became pregnant with my sister Janelle in early 1957. Almost everyone in those days did what was thought to be the right thing when this out-of-wedlock situation arose. Mom and Moe were married in July 1957, and their marriage lasted nearly sixty years before Moe passed in April 2016.

It was at this point in her story when I had another light bulb moment. If at least some version of what she was telling me regarding her relationship with Sonny was partially based in fact, Sonny must have always known I was not his child. That could explain why he never had an interest in a relationship with me. Perhaps he did not want to inflict any ill will toward my mother, because he never told me I was not his child. This spoke well of his character, which conflicted with the character he displayed during some part of our brief conversations.

In hindsight, I am not sure why anything in my life would have concerned him enough that he would even have any discussion with me. I still think I made the right choice to have nothing to do with him after our first phone call based upon his deeply personal questioning of me and his asinine handling of Kerry's lifestyle choice. It is likely that Sonny's sister, Shirley, also knew I was not Sonny's child. That would explain why her answers to my questions were always evasive, why her contact with me was limited, and why she felt there was no need to reach out to me when her husband, her mother, or Sonny passed away.

CHAPTER 16

I Follow the Bread Crumbs

This new information reignited my search with a renewed intensity; however, this time around I was no longer chasing a half-brother. I was trying to find a father. That day certainly went in a direction I never could have imagined. I knew that at my age it might be that I was chasing the grave marker of my father. Now that I had finally identified the Weeks connection, I went back to social media in hopes of finding additional information.

Through Philip's social media site information, I determined that Charles Weeks was his father and Chuckie Weeks was his brother. I stalked Charles Weeks's page and rifled through his timeline. From his available information, I was able to determine that he was younger than I was and would not be the Chuck Weeks my mother had stated was my father. A post from his sister wishing Charles a Happy Siblings Day tagged him along with all his siblings: Denise Weeks Lovell, Cheryl Oncay, Debra Mullis, and Janel (not to be confused with Janelle) Harder. I did a quick check and saw nothing listed for his father.

I searched the page of each sibling for a lead into their parents and found nothing of substance regarding a father. There was a picture on Charles's page with an older man with no caption or tags to identify the males in the photo. Melody saw this same photo during a bit of her own social media timeline reviewing (she prefers that term over *stalking*) and told me she was positive it was a four-generation photo of Charles Weeks Sr., Charles Jr., Chuckie (Charles Jr.'s son), and Chuckie's son.

Things were moving very fast as I processed the information I could glean from each social media site. Coupling that knowledge with the information obtained from previous calls with Theresa and my mother, my mind was a whirlwind of activity as I worked to cover every possible angle of identification. I now had many leads to chase down, and I was trying to determine which would get me to my answer the quickest.

I gave up on social media and moved to the internet phone book to search for a Charles Weeks in Virginia; my hope was to narrow down the little bit of information I had gathered. I chose to look in Virginia because of the location listed for Charles on social media. I thought my best option would be to speak with Charles Weeks Jr. personally, discuss with him what I had found, and see if he could help me put the remaining pieces together.

As with conversations I'd had with Theresa, I hoped discussing possibilities via phone would be the easiest way to dismiss false or incorrect pathways. As he was the father of Philip Tyler Weeks (the ever elusive *philw703*), my hope was he could help me identify our exact family connection. I had many disparate pieces, and I needed the linchpin.

Besides the location for Charles Weeks Jr in Woodbridge, Virginia, the White Pages internet search also provided me the name of Charles Weeks Sr., age eighty-one, with known relatives Janel Harder among others who had lived in Virginia at one time. *Voila!* Eighty-one would be the right age for the father I was trying to chase down. Janel Harder was a sibling to the father of Philip Weeks, my DNA match. I knew I was getting close. The information was aligning almost magically. I was nearly 100 percent certain that I had found the man my mother had identified earlier that morning as my father.

The trail from *philw703* had led to Philip Tyler Weeks to Charles Weeks Jr. to Charles Weeks Sr. Finally! This DNA stuff was amazing. I only needed confirmation from one last source: the man himself.

I was able to find newer listings in the White Pages for several of the siblings and determined that Janel Harder was in Kansas and Charles Sr. was in Georgia. I obtained their phone numbers, although I had no way of ensuring the validity of the information because internet white pages information is not often updated. I did not continue searching for other phone numbers at that time, as I hoped the two I had in hand would be sufficient.

By four o'clock that Saturday afternoon, I had cemented the facts about my relationship to *philw703* and now realized he was my nephew, not my cousin. I also knew exactly where to find Charles Weeks Sr., and I had some major decisions to make.

CHAPTER 17

Questions, Questions, Questions

*H*ow does one contact a parent who knows nothing about him?

I knew I had to be very careful in approaching my father and had to do it in a way that would show him I had no hidden agenda or ulterior motive. I was only interested in an introduction and an open door to whatever relationship he might want to define. That message had to be sincere and conveyed right upfront; I could not impose my needs or my will upon him. Anything beyond the introduction would need to be mutually agreed upon between us for future contact. More than anything else, I wanted there to be honest and open communication. I expected the door to be quickly closed from his end should there be any suspect behavior or words.

*W*hat are the right words to say to start that conversation?

I was sure that, "Hello, Dad," was not the proper greeting. Referring to him as Mr. Weeks felt too formal, although his generation would certainly approve of that more dignified salutation. If my gift of gab has led me anywhere throughout life, it has been to the proper saying for the occasion. However, I could think of no way to take the edge off the surprise the phone call would generate.

I have never been a fan of extemporaneous speaking, and I did not want my initial words to seem practiced or trite. I did not want the approach to seem pushy or too formalized. I felt the words must remain genuine and sincere for there to be any hope of a successful and continuing dialogue. As corny as it might sound, I knew I must speak from my heart.

What expectations do I have?

This is probably the toughest of the questions I asked myself once I determined that I had found my biological father. I did not need a father figure in my life any longer (*need* being the operative word). A fatherly influence to provide perspective in one's life when tough times arise is always good. A fatherly presence to share the good moments in life is always positive. I was not trying to find anyone to help me live. I was simply putting my ancestry together for my descendants, and I hoped for nothing more than acknowledgement and some level of acceptance.

I cannot say for sure why those two things held so much importance for me. I think satisfying my inquisitive mind about who this man is was playing a big role in my expectations.

Am I willing to risk rejection?

As the old saying goes, nothing ventured, nothing gained. I have found rejection to be a normal part of life, and I never sway in my emotional stability when it happens. I am not saying I became immune to the pain it can cause, only that a lifetime of rejections has taught me how to handle and process them while taking them in stride. If my father wanted no future contact between us, I knew I had done all I could from my side and the decision would rest with him.

Is this really what I want to do?

I did not have much time to ponder this. My search of nearly forty years had always focused on a half-brother who was from the Kreider family line. To find a new biological father seemed like a detour instead of a completely new journey. I could think of no logical reason to turn away at that moment, after having spent so much time, energy, and focus fitting the pieces into the puzzle. The short duration of this search was another factor in my decision to answer this question with a resounding yes.

I did not know if it was fate, karma, or divine intervention that led me to this point. I only knew I wanted to go forward. With all the years of searching I had invested thus far, it never occurred to me that I should stop now just because the family connection I was trying to find had changed. I was beyond thankful that the actual outcome had been such an amazing adventure.

*W*hat if he says it's impossible?

I had the DNA proof and the testimonial from my mother that Chuck Weeks was my biological father. Notwithstanding Mom's credibility, there was also the suggestion from my Aunt Faith that Sonny was quite possibly not the correct birth certificate entry. I knew something was off in the Kreider line once I realized no DNA relatives of that family had surfaced in my testing results. It was also evident from my meeting with Mel Jr. that something did not match up in our family tree. I had to believe that anyone even minimally aware of modern DNA capabilities and its reliability could put the information together and come to the same conclusion I had: Charles Weeks Sr. is my biological father.

*W*hat chaos might this cause in his family?

This question is perhaps one of the most important thoughts I considered. If I were the result of anything other than irresponsible activity between two consenting adults, there would be cause for concern. If the situation were clandestine in some fashion, I would have probably had to consider more factors. As it was, there was no spousal cheating involved. There was no surreptitious activity with me as the end result. There was no wrongdoing by anyone. I am simply the result of an unplanned pregnancy. There should be no impact to his family other than knowledge that another descendant exists.

What if it negatively impacts his life?

This would be completely up to him. I had already decided that any contact or further inclusion of me in his life would have to be a mutual decision. Perhaps the decision would land back on my plate once the initial introductions were behind us. I knew nothing of his family, and it was possible they could also negatively affect my life. I decided to accept that risk.

Fortunately, it has not played out that way in any form; however, at the time, that possibility existed. As I had previously reasoned with myself, I neither wanted nor looked for anything more than acknowledgement and acceptance, and if it was going to cause any sort of negative impact on him or his family or me and my family, I could walk away knowing from whom I was descended.

CHAPTER 18

Wrestling with Answers

These were pretty tough questions to answer with no knowledge of the man by which to gauge what his reaction might be. My mother seemed to know very little about Chuck Weeks, but remembered quite vividly that he was always very kind to her and was very intelligent. She professed to know what squadron he worked in at the air base, but was only partially able to identify a name. I am not sure her memory was very accurate on that count. I reasoned I would start with the siblings to get a lay of the land in hopes of obtaining some sort of insight into his demeanor.

Melody and I discussed my concerns about upsetting the balance of his life (and possibly mine). We weighed several options as to how I might best contact him. As always, she gave me nothing but support and encouragement. We decided our primary objective was not to alarm anyone we might reach as we tried to put the final touches on the family connections. After multiple avenues were discussed, we decided an email or instant messaging contact would be the most appropriate and efficient method. We needed to compose an initial greeting with general information and questions that would guarantee a response at the very least and, hopefully, lead to an open discussion.

I went back to social media to search for any additional information about the family. With no email addresses available in their publicly listed information, my option was to reach out to each of the siblings via the social media's private messaging feature. The worst-case scenario would be no responses to my messages. Based upon their timeline postings, it appeared none of the siblings accessed their media accounts regularly, and I was unsure if, or when, any of them might respond. There was also the risk that the siblings would not believe me. This was, after all, an unsolicited message from a stranger in today's environment of social media privacy. There was no basis for them to trust in my information at that point.

I had previously reached out to Philip via a media messenger feature when I first found him with the same outcome I got from the DNA testing service site: he did not answer any messages. I had to trust that it was not a family trait. I found out later that Philip thought I was some nut job trying to contact him for no apparent reason. He had even mentioned it to his dad, Chuck Jr. We had a good laugh about it when we did finally meet. I am sure I will get to tease him about this situation for many more years.

I sent the following private message to each of the siblings:

> Hello. Not trying to be intrusive, so please accept my thanks for taking a moment to review this. My name is Steve and I am tracing down a DNA match on the Weeks side per (a DNA testing site). I am looking for a contact that can tell me if this Weeks family line is right or wrong - not asking for anything else. If you can give me a few minutes to explain how I reached your name, I would be most appreciative. I think a key is a Charles Weeks born about 1936 with family from New Hampshire - if I am incorrect about your connection there, I apologize.

Then came the waiting. I made a couple of wagers with myself about who would respond at all, then guessing which might respond first.

Six o'clock Saturday evening rolled around with no responses. Ten o'clock that night and still none. Midnight ... still none. The same thing was true on Sunday at ten o'clock that morning and two o'clock that afternoon. Where were these people? I told Melody around two thirty on Sunday afternoon that I was still waiting for a response, and we discussed just making a phone call to either of the numbers I had found to get things moving forward. I decided to wait a bit longer and continued hoping one of the siblings would respond to my message.

I debated in my own head about the proper amount of time to wait before deciding to reach out via other contact methods. Was twenty-four hours enough? Why wait at all? For reasons that I did not quite understand, the waiting was torturous. I had been searching for forty-two years, so waiting was nothing new for me. It had been all of one day since I had found out the identity of my biological father, so why was I so impatient? I tried my best to remain calm.

Around four o'clock Sunday afternoon, with my anticipation killing me and a debate raging in my head (sometimes you just cannot ignore the voices!), I decided to abandon the social media private message angle, throw caution to the wind, and just make the phone call. The time for waiting for responses to my private messages was over. It was time to push for a definitive answer.

Because I had two numbers to choose from and I had previously decided to make initial contact with the siblings, my first call was to the number I had for Janel. I dialed it with an odd nervousness and hit an immediate roadblock when I heard a robotic voice on the other end saying, "The number you have dialed has been disconnected." *Dang. Shoot. Now what?*

I had one number left: that of Charles Weeks Sr. Although I could have gone back and looked up phone numbers for the other siblings, I quickly decided that was just as much of an unsure thing as the numbers I had already found. I took a deep breath and dialed the number in Covington, Georgia.

After two rings, a very lovely voice answered, "Hello?"

I simply said, "Hello. My name is Steve Vermeulen, and I am trying to reach Charles Weeks."

The voice replied, "Hold on," and then I heard a new voice—that of the man himself, Charles Weeks Sr.

CHAPTER 19

Dad, Is That You?

I remember having a grand and wonderful conversation with Charles Sr. during that initial phone call; however, many of the specifics elude me. Hindsight tells me I should have taken notes. My adrenaline was intense at the beginning of the call. I remember feeling relief that he did not hang up on me and then feeling great satisfaction that he took the time to speak with me. My nervous energy released quickly as we fell into a very easy conversation.

He listened intently as I mentioned to him that this was going to be one of the strangest calls he had ever received and that I appreciated his time and attention. I went on to explain that I was not selling anything. I was neither looking for nor wanting anything. I just wanted to run some things past him about myself and my past and that it was entirely possible he was my father. There was a brief moment of silence after that last statement ... and then he said, "Well, okay. Let's talk about it." Once we got beyond that short pause, we commenced discussing everything I knew regarding my origins and my reasons for believing he was my father.

I explained he would have met my mother at Otis AFB in early 1955, presumably in February or March based on my birthdate in January 1956. He remembered meeting my mother and her sister (Aunt Faith) while he was stationed on Cape Cod. He validated the time by way of recalling the timeline of his Air Force enlistment in the fall of 1954, home from basic training for Christmas 1954, then sent to tech school in Mississippi for six weeks, and then shipped to Otis AFB in February 1955.

He told me he had dated my mother only few times. Actually, he used the term *affair*, which had a different meaning back in that era than it does today. Mom later explained that *dating* back then meant just dating, but an *affair* meant dating with intimate relations. Chuck Sr. did not indicate any reason as to why they stopped seeing each other. I do not know if he did not recall the reason or if he simply thought it unnecessary to explain.

I told him about my DNA testing and the family relationships I had been able to confirm. I mentioned Philip Tyler Weeks as the first Weeks descendant I had identified from my DNA results. He confirmed that Philip was his grandson. After we discussed the series of events and details as he recalled them compared to the information I had been able to uncover, he agreed that, indeed, he was my father.

It is possible the thoroughness of the information I had accumulated perhaps impressed him because he had been in private investigations and law enforcement (civilian and military) for most of his adult life.

We talked for about twenty minutes, during which time he told me he had been married for fifty-seven years to his wife, Ellon, and they had five children. There was some general discussion about each of our lives. For me, the most poignant point he made was when he told me they were a loving family and that he wanted to be the first to welcome me into it.

He was clearly very proud of his children and their characters. He assured me my new siblings would be welcoming when they found out about me. He told me, "You'll enjoy them," and I found that to be very true once we did finally meet.

Toward the end of the conversation, I promised to reach out to him again and gave him my contact information. I remember having the thought that he would not call me, but I hoped he would want to keep in touch. I promised myself I would call again in a few weeks and test those waters. It was a truly wonderful conversation. At no moment did I feel that he was anything other than supportive of our conversation and accepting of our new reality.

I wish I had recorded that call to use as a training lesson for other fathers who might one day find themselves in this sort of situation. He could not have been more understanding or kind throughout our entire conversation.

I told Melody about the call later that afternoon, and she was very excited that I had received such a welcoming and positive reaction. I still had not heard from any of the siblings from my private messages, but that was secondary now as I had the confirmed answer—yes, he was my father. I would try to reach the siblings another time if for no other reason than to say hello. There were many questions filling my mind as the realization set in that I had a completely new reality to traverse.

CHAPTER 20

I Ask Myself More Questions

What would the new siblings think of this situation?

Chuck Sr. had explained that the five children ranged in age from late forties to middle fifties with a difference of seven years between the youngest and the oldest. This put all of them in the late sixties and early seventies era of Let's all love one another and be free. Because I would not become involved with his family if not invited inside their lives, they had no reason to be concerned about me. Until I spoke with each of them regarding my existence, they would not know I posed no threat. It did not occur to me that he could be embarrassed for them to learn about my existence because I did not see an embarrassing aspect to any part of the situation. I found out later that he did feel some embarrassment, although unwarranted, as if this situation would somehow tarnish his reputation.

Would they truly be okay with the knowledge of me as Chuck Sr. had assured?

I sincerely hoped that answer would be yes. There are families who are protective of their core members and the places they hold within the family hierarchy. I knew it was possible there could be questions or concerns about any motives I might have (I had none) as a new member who had suddenly come out of the woodwork.

If I had known about the Weeks family for years and had only just then chosen to come forward, this sentiment would be understandable. This simply was not the situation, and I bore the responsibility to make the siblings feel as comfortable and unthreatened as possible. The absolute truth was that I posed no threat and had no ill intentions. Their reaction upon learning about me was better than I could ever have hoped. They have been incredibly welcoming to Melody and me at every turn.

Would their lives change and how?

When you think about changes in life, the change is only going to be what each person allows. While my intent was to enhance the life of my father and siblings with my entry into their close-knit family, I was not so naïve or egotistical as to think I would make that difference.

I decided early in the process that I would only be as involved as the new family wanted me to be. I would be there as they needed me, if they so choose. I thought it would be wonderful to double the size of my family, and I hoped to be up to the challenge. It was, and still is, my sincerest hope that I do not cause any negative impact.

In an odd thought, it also occurred to me that I had gone from being the only brother among four children to the oldest brother among nine children. It also occurred to me that I no longer had any full siblings. I was a half-sibling to all eight. This may be a non-issue for many, but it did cause me to lean to the little bit freaked out side. I was very excited and very much amazed by the unfolding events.

The gamut of emotions that enveloped me was vast, rapid, and daunting. I can recall being almost mesmerized, if not slightly overwhelmed, by how mentally consuming the weekend had been. From being told about my new father to be having immediately successful search results to opening a new door into my future by reaching out and being accepted by a new family, my weekend had left me smiling with an odd sense of calmness. Melody and I tried going about our normal Sunday routines as best we could, despite the sense of amazement at what the weekend had brought forth. It was all we could talk about for the remainder of that day and many days after.

CHAPTER 21

A Sibling Responds

Sometime after dinner that Sunday evening while I was sitting at my computer reading some online news articles, Denise became the first of my new siblings to respond to my private social media message.

She said that Charles was her father, confirmed he was born in 1936 in New Hampshire, and asked what I needed. I asked her to call me because it would be far easier to explain during a conversation than via the messenger app. I had hardly completed typing in my home phone number when the phone rang.

Wow! What excitement I was met with as I told her my story, all the way from the beginning to when my DNA results were delivered. I explained how I got to her name through media searches and that I'd already had my questions about our connection answered. I further explained that I had confirmed my connection to the Weeks family in a conversation with her father earlier in the day.

Then I told her I was his son and her brother. With that statement, the tone of our conversation changed dramatically. There were many *OMG* moments. I should repeat that—many *OMG* moments and many *this-is-great* comments. I received nothing but excitement and unconditional welcoming from her.

We had a wonderful back-and-forth question and answer session. There were never any "Are you sure?" types of questions; only agreement with all the information I provided. Once Denise had the specifics on the information about me and my earlier discussion with Chuck Sr., she promised to get back in touch after she shared the news with her brother and sisters. She said she needed to end our call and would start calling them right away. Denise assured me they would all be very excited by the news and what a wonderful surprise the call with me had been.

For me, it was a completely overwhelming acceptance. Truth be told, I was very appreciative of her excitement and enthusiasm regarding my out-of-the-blue arrival.

CHAPTER 22

We Begin Telling Friends and Family

My first call was to my son, Christopher. I worried this new family plot twist might be difficult for him to hear and accept because family is so important to him. I'd already had a discussion with him years earlier regarding Dad and the real (or so I thought at the time) last name we shared. I told him when I went through the legal name change and the ramifications to him (of which, as I understood it, there were none) for the Vermeulen/Kreider ancestry. To bring another name into the mix could have been difficult information for him to receive. I wanted to be sure that he did not feel any disappointment toward his grandmother for the events of so long ago. His name is verifiably Vermeulen, and his son, Eli, holds the same name.

I was relieved to find that Christopher was great with the news. While he was certainly as surprised as I had been, he was truly excited to have more family connections. He seemed particularly excited to learn one of my siblings (his new, and now favorite, Aunt Janel) lived just a couple of hours away from his home in Missouri and is married to a real-life rancher who works a three-thousand-acre cattle ranch. Having another cousin in the family was also extra special to Christopher. I suspect he will be a welcome visitor in their home on many occasions.

We are extremely fortunate to have many good friends around

us, and we wanted to share this news with all of them. Melody sent texts to two of our closest friends, Andrea and Beth. As we met up with other members of our friend group as time went on, we related the story, the journey, and the mesmerizing outcome that was so wonderful. I say *we* because Melody was just as excited about this turn of events as I was. We talked about the newfound family to almost anyone who would listen whether it be our friends, coworkers, hairdressers, or a random person in line behind us at a grocery store. I had received a summons for jury duty in late July and talked about it to complete strangers during breaks from the courtroom. I spent an entire heart stress test walking on the treadmill at my cardiologist's office discussing the story with the attending nurses.

Everyone was amazed. Kind words and wonderment abounded. Nobody we encountered had any relatable story; we began realizing just how unique and special our experience had become. We continue to tell the story repeatedly and still marvel at the awesome outcome. We hope others in similar situations get the same experience.

A few days later, I told my mother I had found Chuck Weeks Sr. I explained he was living in Georgia, just a short daytrip south of my current home. She responded to the facts I shared regarding how I found him, and his marriage and family, stoically with only an occasional "hmmm" or "I see." It seemed to me that she was still not happy with me for pursuing my biological father and family. Maybe she was experiencing some guilt over telling me about Chuck so late in my life. Maybe she was trying to figure out how she would explain the situation to my sister, Janelle, with whom she resided.

I found out later that my sense of her displeasure was correct and that it was all about her in her own mind. She held an idea that the new family would be an adjunct to her in some fashion. As an example, when I informed her that I would be arranging a meeting with Chuck Sr. and the siblings, she wanted me to be sure to have a current and flattering picture of her to present. She was upset when I explained to her that the meeting would not be about her, and that I was not going to show the family her picture unless they inquired and insisted. I felt that flashing a picture of an old girlfriend would be disrespectful to Ellon. She had been married to Chuck Sr. for fifty-seven years. She had raised a family with him. She did not need a reminder of someone who was part of his life long before she met him. This journey was real and about me, not about some fantasy that my mom may have created in her mind.

Two days after telling my mother about the search results, I discussed my new family with my sister, Janelle. I was not sure what spin Mom might have put on the story or if she had brought up the subject to Janelle at all. I mentioned previously, and will note again as a refresher, that Mom has a way of not being completely forthcoming in many situations. I was concerned that Janelle would feel left out or was provided a wrong impression and incomplete information about my family search results. She has always been my closest sibling in thoughts and actions, and I did not want to jeopardize her feelings in any way.

It turned out Mom had mentioned the story to her, but not in the same detail that I had provided. She was very excited when I gave her the whole story, and that was a tremendous relief for me. Her support was immediate. She reveled in the craziness as I explained all the work I had done to get to the truth. We chuckled about me having two sisters with the same name (spelled differently) and made some Who's your daddy? jokes. The conversation with Janelle was great.

During the call, I asked her to keep a close eye on Mom because of what she may have endured emotionally with the revelation of a secret she had held so closely for so long and was a bit embarrassing for her. Mom was obviously quite shaken over the entire situation per her reactions during the phone calls I had with her. I was worried she might tailspin into some pattern of depression while she processed the events and whatever remorse she might be feeling after divulging this secret.

I thought it best to allow Mom to tell my youngest sister, Brenda, in her own time and her own way. Brenda and I had suffered with a rather strained relationship for the previous four or so years due to my family decisions. This, understandably, resulted in a few hurt feelings, causing Brenda and I to begin a long period of estrangement. Telling her about my newfound birth father myself, while certainly my initial preference, would have been a challenge simply because of how infrequently we communicated at that moment in time.

When several months had passed and Brenda had not once broached the subject during our infrequent meetings, it occurred to me that maybe Mom had decided to not tell Brenda or, perhaps,

Brenda knew and thought it might be too awkward of a subject to bring up to me directly. If Mom had not told her, I felt Brenda had a right to know what the rest of us knew, and I needed to decide when and how best to tell her.

If she knew about the situation and perhaps felt any awkwardness, I wanted to explain that I was okay with the knowledge of who my birth father was as well as the events that followed and how it had ultimately enriched my life. I wanted to assure her there was no reason for her to be cautious when speaking with me about this—or about anything else.

CHAPTER 23

We Must Get Together

I thought a group call would be a great way to get to know my new family as quickly as possible. I chose to arrange a conference bridge for my siblings, their spouses, and their families as a way to introduce myself to everyone at once. Plans were made with Denise to have all the siblings gather on the call a week after our initial discussion on a Sunday evening. Denise handled the coordinating on the Weeks side. Melody and I were the only attendees from my side. I opted not to involve Chuck Sr. and Ellon in this first group call because I'd already had my initial conversation with him and was unsure, at that point, if Ellon knew of my existence.

I was very much anticipating the group call with the siblings. Fortunately, any nervousness was eased by text messages from Denise and Chuck Jr., as well as a few short phone calls with Denise throughout the week leading up to the group call. Getting them all together on a call would be another step in this wonderful journey to Weeks family acceptance.

When Sunday evening finally arrived, I opened the bridge call with minimal concerns and high expectations. The call lasted for more than ninety minutes. The time seemed to fly by so fast. There were tons of questions about many life matters, discussions of locations and families, and much laughter about the circumstances surrounding the events of the past week. There were stories of upbringing and our father's expectations. There were sentiments of thankfulness shared about the timing of my contact with the family. There was genuine concern expressed for the deep feelings that were suddenly surfacing for all the parties involved. So many more *OMG* moments occurred amid the conversation.

At some point during the call, Denise or Cheryl mentioned that Ellon knew about me and had discussions with them about how wonderful the news was. We also found out that Melody and I were not the only ones who were talking about my arrival to anyone and everyone who would listen. Their interest and attention made me feel so very special. My introduction to this family was so different from the family experiences of my childhood. I am a member accepted into their family without question. I no longer felt like an outsider in my own skin.

The discussion was such a whirlwind that I missed many things such as birthdays and spouses' and children's names. I knew I would need to catch that information the next time when my head stopped spinning from the pace of the events. Throughout the call, there was a noticeable affinity among the siblings. So much laughter and good-natured ribbing took place over life events that I could tell future family gatherings would be a colossal hoot. Each of the siblings had stories to share, and the others would chime in with their take on the situations.

I could tell that having another brother in the mix would be a great benefit to Chuck Jr. because the girls could not gang up on him as easily as prior times. I was heartened to have been so warmly welcomed by each of them and their families. Toward the end of the call, we made plans for an in-person meeting—not one dissenting vote, not one cautious tale, and zero hesitancy across the board. They wanted to meet us as much as we wanted to meet them.

Melody and I are within easy driving distance of most of my new family. We live just four and a half hours south of my new brother and seven hours north of my new father, step-mother, and three of my sisters. One sister lives in Kansas within a couple of hours of my son and grandson. Chuck Jr. suggested a meeting in Georgia as soon as possible due to the relative ages and infirmities of those involved. The weekend beginning August 4th would the first available time that Chuck Jr. and his wife, Brenda, would be able to travel. Melody and I would drive to Georgia where we would meet up with as many of the family as could make it into Covington that weekend. Those not able to be there would have to settle for pictures of the gathering.

We filled the three weeks between the group call and the in-person meeting with many separate calls and texts with my new siblings. Melody and Chuck Jr. handled the planning of where best to get a hotel, where we could meet the sisters locally, and the overall trip organization. I was in a bit of a euphoric fog on most days as I tried to get a good handle on my new family lineage. Some disappointment with my mother's handling of the situation also began to fester within me.

As I learned more about the Weeks family and felt how kind and welcoming they had been to Melody and me, I grew more discontented with the idea of what I had been missing for so much of my life. There were days I had to talk myself off the proverbial ledge as I processed and resolved those feelings. I eventually determined there was nothing to gain from lingering on the past and resolved to look forward to the promising family get-together.

CHAPTER 24

Meeting Time Has Arrived!

The first new sibling I met was Chuck Jr. along with his wife, Brenda. They had already arrived at the hotel where we were all going to stay and came down to the lobby to greet us as we were checking in for that much-anticipated weekend. It was straight-up awesome with hugs and smiles all around. Comfort. Such a comfortable presence. Denise and Cheryl joined us at the hotel a short while later, and we spent a wonderful few hours chatting. I remember smiling so much. I remember them smiling just as much.

We went to dinner and continued talking about the journey that resulted in me finding this new family. Again, there were many smiles. I do not think I have smiled that much or that continuously ever in my life. We went back to the hotel after dinner for more chatting with many more smiles. I do not have the words to sum up the afternoon and evening other than to say it was just a wonderful and awesome time. We spent at least seven hours together that first evening talking, dining, and then talking some more. I was amazed at how quickly the time flew by. I would not trade a single minute of that first evening away.

There was a lot of curiosity about me and discussions about my mannerisms. I had, understandably, a lot of curiosity about the new family as well. I used the term *shit for brains* while discussing something during that first evening, and Cheryl and Denise nearly fell out of their chairs. Apparently, Chuck Sr. used that exact same phrase quite often and they had never heard it used by anyone other than him.

We discussed other characteristics and nuances that I seemed to have in common with Chuck Sr. I always carry a cloth handkerchief with me. I have a similar speech cadence. I have some odd food tastes that are uncannily similar. I have some OCD mannerisms that are also spot-on identical. We had hours of conversation throughout that great evening and so much laughter.

Saturday was all about hanging out together, getting to know each other, and touring the quaint town of Covington. We discovered the area had a lot of history, which was very interesting to learn about for this longtime Midwestern couple. The best part was the experience of being with our new family. We just kept talking and learning about each other and enjoying the company. The day was full of sunshine, smiles, light breezes, cool weather, and family. I am not sure what could have made it any better—maybe the faint whisper of a calliope playing in the distance. (Oh, stop. This is reality, not the movies!)

We had plans for Saturday evening August 5th to meet Chuck Sr. and Ellon for dinner at one of their favorite family-style Italian restaurants. During our Saturday meanderings, I curiously felt neither nervous nor concerned about the dinner meeting. I think the credit for much of that goes to Chuck Jr. We talked a lot about how Chuck Sr. might be feeling about the pending meeting. This was such a new experience, and there was no handbook for how either of us might handle our initial meeting.

I can admit to having moments of doubt about how to make the meeting successful. Fortunately, those moments passed upon deep introspection. I went to dinner thinking that there was nothing to worry about because he was likely as excited about the meeting as I was. How often do you get to meet a relative for the first time in sixty-one years?

I later learned that Chuck Sr. was a bit intrigued, but also a bit reluctant, over the prospect of meeting me. I credit Chuck Jr. again with helping his dad overcome that obstacle through some very intense and personal conversations between them. I also found out that after our Friday get-together, Cheryl and Denise had gone to Chuck Sr. and Ellon's home and told them about how great our afternoon and evening had been. Denise and Cheryl were also quite involved in ensuring Chuck Sr. was comfortable and willing to attend the initial meeting. Apparently, he held some concerns that he had failed me in some way for reasons he did not disclose. Denise had shared with us recently that he had said to her, "There's just no way that I can ever make it up to him."

Denise assured him that there was nothing for him to make up; neither of us had done anything wrong because neither of us knew of the other's existence. The result was that Chuck Sr. came to dinner, and we finally met one another as father and son.

CHAPTER 25

After Sixty-One Years, Father and Son Meet at Last

*M*y first sighting of Chuck Sr. was in the restaurant parking lot. I recall Chuck Jr. pointing out their car as we were searching for a parking space. Ellon and Chuck Sr. had just gotten out of their vehicle when I caught the first sight of my father. During our walk across the parking lot, it appeared Cheryl and Denise were pointing me out to him as they also awaited our arrival just outside the restaurant front door. Chuck Sr. had decided to wait outside and make our introduction right there in front of the restaurant.

It was an honor to share his firm handshake. He mentioned that seeing me walking across the parking lot with Chuck Jr. reminded him of walking alongside his brother, Philip, years earlier.

The meeting and dinner could not have been orchestrated any better. Chuck Sr. motioned for me to sit next to him almost by command (which I later learned was his way). There seemed to be no awkwardness at all. We had a lot to discuss during dinner, especially about the sudden discovery and subsequent flurry of activities once our family connection was uncovered. At some point, I explained to Chuck Sr. that he had known about me for just one day less than I had known about him. Our mutual respect grew as the first hour progressed. Chuck Sr. asked about many aspects of my life, such as education and work. His interest in my life was genuine.

He was quite interested in my career. He was interestingly curious as to why I had never completed an advanced college degree given my line of work in the high-tech world of data connectivity. He explained a few of his interests and again repeated that he wished he had known about me. I assured him there was no reason to worry about the past, as we were moving ahead.

The conversations around the table were as easy and natural as that of any long-together family. I gained some insights into the closeness of the family as they shared the first of many long-held family stories and moments of humor and fun times from their history. I answered all the questions from the family as simply as I could—this was a new world order for me, and I was intent to have no secrets kept hidden. They, in turn, answered any question I posed without concern or hesitation.

Several words that come to mind about the dinner and conversation could never cover the evening events. Incredible graciousness would cover it best. Every step I have taken with the Weeks family has been met with grace and kindness.

My father was not the only member of the family I met at that initial dinner. There was also Ellon, my new step-mother. I would be remiss if I did not take a moment to acknowledge Ellon for the wonderful and warm welcome she has given Melody and me. What a gentle, kind, and lovely spirit she is.

She has accepted Melody and I without hesitation, and there is no amount of thanks available to repay her. Her kind words and constant smile are welcome insights into her beautiful soul. She took the time to pass along some words of wisdom about the past to me at dinner. She told me if I was holding any resentment toward my mother for keeping this secret, I should not because "times were very different back then."

An invitation to come back to the family home capped off the evening. Just as he had at dinner, Chuck Sr. pointed me to a chair next to his, and we settled in at their home to continue getting to know one another.

We had a great few hours of talking and discovery. We discussed many more aspects of my life, and he discussed many more of his interests and hobbies. He was very proud to share his life accomplishments with me and help me understand the man I now knew was truly my father. There was never a feeling of worry over any aspect of this journey or the information discussed. I was a full-blown member of his family, and everyone shared with me as if I had been with them my entire life.

I continue to revel in amazement at how pleasant the entire event was. Character abounds in this family, starting with Chuck Sr. and Ellon and flowing through their entire family. Shortly before we left to go back to the hotel, my father said to me, "Now when someone asks me how many children I have, I'll have to tell them six."

We ended the weekend on a very high note. I cannot overstate how comfortable the entire weekend was from start to finish. The smiles shared were innumerable, and the family dynamic that evolved could not possibly have been better. Our departure Sunday morning to head back to Raleigh was slightly bittersweet. The awesome visit had ended—when could we have another?

CHAPTER 26

Oh No, Surely Not

My wonderful ride took a tragic turn just a few weeks later on August 28th. I had spoken to Chuck Jr. on my way home from work that day at about five o'clock, just keeping in touch so we could continue growing as brothers. Around eleven o'clock that night, Chuck called me at home. I thought he was remembering something from the earlier call and was going to throw in a brotherly dig. Unfortunately, that was not the case. I knew very quickly that something was wrong when he said he was sorry to have to make this call to me. Sadly, he was calling to tell me our father had passed away a little earlier in the evening.

My immediate thoughts were how sorry I was for the family, and most especially for the man I now called a brother. I had lost a dad of sixty years just over a year earlier, and I fully understood the sadness they were feeling. My next thoughts were just a repeat of *wow* and *damn*. Things had been so good and so positive, and then reality sets in. Things are still good and positive, but now a hugely important part was missing.

Melody and I made a solemn second trip back to Georgia less than a month after that wonderful first trip and meeting. I will admit to feeling somewhat snake bit about my circumstance. To have found (thankfully) and then lost (unfortunately) my biological father so quickly was difficult to accept. Yet while I would not have the chance to learn more about Chuck Sr. from our own personal conversations, I would now have the grand opportunity to hear about his wonderful life accomplishments, his deeply held family convictions, and his vast array of deep-seated friendships during the first evening at the funeral home. The exposure was a crash course that left me even more sorrowful for my late introduction into Chuck Sr.'s life.

Everyone I spoke with during the visitation evening reinforced Chuck Sr.'s outstanding character for me. His friends and family members shared many a tale as they helped me learn more about the man my father was to each of them. I hope I was helping them deal with the loss of someone who seemed to have been so instrumental in their own lives by being there to appreciate their stories. I thank them all and appreciate their effort to find goodness within their grief. He was a very beloved man.

I learned of his zest for Christmas parties and his special fondness for bingo. His friends spoke of circumstances and stories that had been told numerous times and still cause laughter and guffaw at every mention. Each of his friends had their own special memory to share with me—that is a tribute to how Chuck Sr. could make each person feel special in his or her own way.

The visitation at the funeral home was where I was finally able to meet my other two sisters, Janel and Debra, in person. That was a positive experience in a very sad setting. I wished the circumstances of our meeting were far different than they were, but I was grateful that we were able to finally meet face-to-face. I looked forward to many more meetings in more festive surroundings. The evening was busy with many introductions as I met a large portion of the extended family for the first time. There was overall happiness and awe of my arrival into the family that mixed in with the sorrow surrounding the moment.

I met relatives from Ellon's side of the family, longtime friends of the family, cousins, and great-nieces and great-nephews. I told the story of how my search led to this family discovery multiple times. Melody and I experienced acceptance at every turn. The kind welcome we received from everyone contrasted with the deep reverence and sorrow everyone shared for the man they had just lost. That so many had turned out to pay their respects to Chuck Sr. that night and the next day at his funeral was a tribute to his far-reaching life. Seeing the sheer number of family and friends, I knew it would take me some time to understand how his life intersected with and affected them all.

CHAPTER 27

Honoring a Life Well Lived

The morning of the funeral was gray and drizzly. The gloomy and wet forecast was a stark contrast to the normally bright and warm late summer weather of the area. Arriving at the funeral home early with Chuck and Brenda allowed a few minutes of quiet time to gather in a small group and speak with some close family friends. It was heartening to find out the family was handling the situation well based on discussions with their friends as more folks arrived for the service. Soon enough, we were ushered into the chapel area.

Music filled the chapel as the service began with some surprising choices given the circumstance –*A Hundred Pounds of Clay* was played early into the service; soon after we hear ABBA. Yes. ABBA was playing! *Dancing Queen* ... really? I am not sure I would have ever guessed, but that was one of Chuck Sr.'s favorite songs. Melody and I were truly impressed.

The service was full of stories shared from the pulpit about some bygone exploits inked into memories, recollections of trips, smiles and laughter, and heartfelt tributes to the good deeds and friendships Chuck Sr. carried throughout his years. While everyone was reliving those wonderful moments together, I was learning so much more about my father.

Soon after the beginning of the service, I realized I had made a judgement error for which I can only blame myself. I did not seek Melody's advice as I should. As I mentioned earlier in this story, I always carry a cloth handkerchief, and that day was no different.

Well, maybe just slightly different because instead of having one, I had four in various pockets of my suit. I thought I would have one for Ellon in case she would need it, one for myself because I find my own emotions and feelings are closer to the surface as I get older and was sure to be touched by the events of that day, one for Melody, and one spare for whomever might need it.

I simply did not have enough handkerchiefs. I should have had at least six with me ... and maybe more. There was a step-mother, four sisters, a wife, a sister-in-law, a brother, and I who all needed to blot a tear. I needed to up my game now that my family was so much larger. I did try to make up for my error later at the home gathering by giving a handkerchief to the sisters I had missed, but I still felt terrible. I vowed to myself never to be short of handkerchiefs again. If there was a good thing that came from it, the hankies are now mementos—a little piece from me that might give a bit of solace and remembrance.

Chuck Sr.'s interment was at the Georgia National Cemetery in Canton, about a ninety-minute drive from the funeral home. The procession to the cemetery was led by two motorcycle police officers in very wet conditions through the mad traffic of Atlanta's highway and interstate system. Those fine officers did an amazing job of stopping heavy traffic and keeping the long line of mourners moving through the maze of commuters. Uncaring or unthinking drivers interrupted the procession several times. Each time the officers would handle the situation with stern efforts and directions to the offenders.

Either there is a loss of respect from drivers for funeral processions, or the proper etiquette is unknown to new drivers. Whichever it is, the opposite was true as we turned off the highways from Atlanta and onto the final route through Canton, Georgia.

Drivers along the highway stopped and allowed the procession to pass in a show of respect. Not just one or two—all of them. We traversed many miles of highway near Canton, and the result was unanimous. There were many respectful drivers in that last stretch leading to the cemetery entrance, and I thank them all.

The final act for our escort team was a stop at the entrance to the cemetery and a well-postured salute as the hearse and mourners passed through the gates to Chuck Sr.'s final resting place of honor.

The graveside military Honor Guard was impressive from most any perspective. The clearing of the skies for a brief period when we arrived at the Honor Guard Memorial was the bonus of the day. The Honor Guard was flawless in their cadence and skill: the movement of the casket, the placement of the guards, and the handling of the US flag. Nothing but pure perfection as they bid final honors to a military man of distinction. I thought it was befitting when the Sergeant of the Guard asked all active and former military members to present arms during one portion of the ceremony. As a veteran myself, I was proud to accompany my fellow veterans in saluting the farewell. The twenty-one-gun salute and the playing of *Taps* were both solemn and moving reminders of the occasion.

After removing the US flag from the casket and folding it in the Triangle of Rights, Privileges, and Freedoms, the Honor Guard presented it to Ellon with the most incredible display of dignity and respect. The ceremony was not a lengthy one, but it will hold a long-lasting impression on all who attended. I have been to several military funerals in my time, and this one was perhaps the one most personal.

CHAPTER 28

Family Fellowship and Future Plans

We departed the cemetery once the final guests had left the memorial ceremony area. I had some time to learn more about the fun my new family enjoys together when we made a quick stop for a late lunch in Canton before heading back to the family home in Covington. Melody and I listened to tales about some road trips the family endured as we discussed the upcoming long ride back to the family house. We were regaled with a lot of the situations Chuck Sr. put the family through, causing laughter and joy. Internally, I noted additional mannerisms and traits discussed that seemed to be genetic. Melody knows which ones, but our shared sense of direction will probably hit home when she reads the entirety of this story.

During our drive back to Covington, Melody and I decided we would stop at the hotel to change into more casual clothing for the afternoon and evening with the family; plus, I had the ulterior motive of picking up more handkerchiefs to try and make amends for my earlier faux pas. We knew we would be at the family house for most of the evening to support the family, and comfortable clothing is always our preference. When we arrived at the house later that afternoon, we found we were not the only ones who had chosen the casual dress option, and I was able to deliver the extra handkerchiefs along with my best hugs and apologies.

That evening and the following day were a recollection of the recent events. We spent many hours engaged in wonderful conversations with newly met nieces, nephews, and friends. There were discussions about the crazy traffic procession and the way the escort team handled the unruly and disrespectful drivers. There were chuckles about some of the hilarious stories during the funeral service. There was awe at the dignity of the cemetery service. There were more recaps of my story to those few family members I had not already had the pleasure to engage. The atmosphere remained solemn, yet light, as the new reality of the future loomed ahead.

There were a few mementos handed out for special remembrances of Chuck Sr., and I was the proud recipient of a photograph of the airplane he worked aboard during his time at Otis AFB, as well as a model version of the same craft. I have it displayed in my dining room to this day. One of the highlights of that evening for me was sitting and speaking with my Uncle Philip for an extended period. I found his stories and knowledge very interesting and intriguing. Melody and I must get to New Hampshire and spend a little time on his turf.

There were pictures taken of Chuck Jr., Uncle Philip, and me chatting at the table. Much like pictures taken of Chuck and me with our father at that first dinner, those pictures will be forever treasured.

The siblings all agreed that I look like Uncle Philip from their first sight of me in pictures on my social media page. They set up side-by-side photos for comparison of us at similar ages, and while the likeness was easily identifiable to others, I did not see the same resemblance as quickly. I seemed to be the only one who did not share the universally held opinion. I did think that, if it was true, Uncle Philip and I sure are handsome devils.

There were several pictures taken with us side–by-side throughout the visitation and post-funeral gathering. While reviewing the pictures afterward, I had to go with the prevailing opinion and agree the resemblance was there. I do, indeed, look like Uncle Philip. It was said that when I am standing side by side with Chuck Jr., we resemble pictures of our father standing side by side with Philip as younger men, and I consider that a wonderful comparison.

We had made plans to leave for home Saturday morning and give the family time alone to open discussions for the future without Chuck Sr. I was unsure what plans were set to handle the multitude of situations that arise when a family patriarch has passed. I did not feel I was in any place to join in the decisions because I was a new addition to the family. I could offer suggestions about a few issues having gone through this a year earlier with my step-father, but I did not intend to butt in. I can happily say I was not in a position where that came into play. As I have also previously stated several times, I was included in the discussions without concern, and I never felt out of place or unwelcome. The family planned to provide Ellon as much attention as she needed or wanted; her well-being was at the center of their concerns.

Because I had finally met Janel and Debra during this trip, I was able to spend a little more time with each of them in the family setting. We had some wonderful conversations. They added to the stories of past hysterical moments from the family archives. I was just as enthralled to meet them and hear about their lives as I had been with Denise, Cheryl, and Chuck. We had too little time to do much one-on-one talking, but I am going to work hard on that in the future.

Each of us has a perspective and getting to know the family means learning all the perspectives. I know there will be many more times we can get together and fill those empty pages.

CHAPTER 29

The Siblings Are Gathered

This is one of the first pictures taken with all of the siblings. The camera must have been on a slant because I am sure Chuck Jr. is slightly taller than I am. This angle has an optical illusion.

CHAPTER 30

Two DNA Services Agree

*U*pon learning that Chuck Sr., Chuck Jr., and Cheryl had previously submitted their samples to another DNA service, I opted to do the same for further confirmation. We would be in the same database once the analysis was complete. Because the DNA services do not share information between their companies, I would recommend that anyone looking for a family member consider using more than one DNA testing provider.

The DNA results were just another confirmation of what we all now knew, as my results in the second provider's system listed Cheryl Oncay as a half-sister and Charles Weeks Jr. as a half-brother. I cannot imagine what my reaction (or theirs) would have been upon receiving email notifications of new DNA matches if had I opted to do the second testing service first instead of the one I chose. The eventual outcome would have been the same, of course, but I would have had additional time to get to know Chuck Sr. better instead of just our one get-together.

I am thankful we got to the chance to meet when we did. Chuck Sr.'s DNA results were not initially open to the public, though Cheryl eventually shared his results with me. To my distinct pleasure, Charles Weeks Sr. is now shown in my DNA family roster as my father ... as it should be.

I continue to feel honored by my new family's acceptance as a late-arriving addition. My life has been changed and improved forever, and I sincerely hope my new family connections feel the same. I think nothing could sum it up better than this quote from my sister Cheryl: *"It's just like seeing a brother we have not talked to in a while."*

To me, that feels a lot like welcome home.

CHAPTER 31

Positive Notes

During our initial phone conversation, Chuck Sr. had asked me if my mother was still living, to which I replied, Yes. He asked if I would give her a message the next time I spoke to her. I thought I should hear the message before deciding if I could deliver it verbatim. The message was that she should have told him about the pregnancy, and he would have done the right thing. I knew right then the character of this man was solid, and he would never have abandoned me.

He did not know that her situation at the time dictated she could not have done the right thing, so to speak, as she was married (albeit separated) when she met and dated him. I promised him I would deliver the message, although I chose to edit it just a bit. I only told her he had asked me to deliver the message that she should have told him. I felt including the "done the right thing" portion was moot at that point.

I was baptized in the Catholic church, brought up in a Methodist church, attended a non-denominational Christian church, converted to a Lutheran church for my first wife, and am married to a Baptist second wife, and DNA tells me I am 12 percent Jewish. I am probably just giving up any designated religious affiliation and hoping for the best.

Before we returned to Covington for Chuck Sr.'s funeral in late August, Melody and I had already made plans to visit Kansas in mid-September to meet Janel and her family. We had plans in place to visit Des Moines, Iowa, during September to see my mother and my sisters,

Janelle and Brenda, as well as visit Kansas City, Missouri, to visit my son and grandson. It would be simple to make a side trip to Junction City, Kansas, to meet Janel and her family who were only a two hour drive from Kansas City, Missouri. We added an extra day to the trip, allowing time for the drive to meet them.

We completed the trip as planned and had the most wonderful time with Janel, her family, and her closest friends. I am astonished at the kindness surrounding my newfound family and everyone around them. I have heard that kindness begets kindness, and this experience has been living proof of that.

CHAPTER 32

The Best Accidental Family One Could Ask For

Chuck and Brenda have been real stalwarts for us. They have been able to answer questions about the family, give a history lesson or two about family matters, help us understand the vast array of friends the family has, and provide tour guide services around the Georgia area.

In the unfortunate circumstance of the funeral, we were able to meet his sons, Chuckie (along with his wife, Sarah, and their son) and Philip (remember the *philw703* who never answered any contact queries?), who are all great—again, more awesome and welcoming family. Chuck and Brenda have visited our home several times now, and we have visited them in Virginia; we look forward too many, many more visits. We keep in touch often, but no less than biweekly and usually more often than that. It has been great having a brother. The sisters are all very cool, but a brother is a new experience for both of us. I am sure we will have many opportunities for get-togethers, and I hope the same happens with my new sisters.

We enjoyed a weekend vacation in early October 2017 in Pigeon Forge, Tennessee, with our friends Art and Kathy. Ellon, Denise, and Cheryl made the trip up from Georgia to stay a few days and meet us for dinner and a half day of shopping and being tourists. This was extraordinary to me—they made the trip to see us. Just because we were going to be someplace, they came, too. Wow. I am truly a lucky man to have found that I am part of such a loving family. The cards could have fallen in such a different fashion. I am so glad they did not!

I now have two sisters named Janelle—different spelling, but same pronunciation. That will take some adjustment; for now, we refer to them as Janelle and New Janel. I have a sister and a sister-in-law both named Brenda. Both my new sister Debra and I have sons named Christopher.

The ease and comfort around us as we engage with the family cannot be overstated. There has been full acceptance from the beginning. The conversations are honest and unguarded. The welcome is sincere. The love is unconditional. All are things I am thankful to have received, and all contribute to the grand sense of belonging I feel. I believe Chuck Sr. would be very proud of his family for their part in making this experience positive. I can only hope my new family will be as proud of me as they are of each other.

I cannot think of a single person Melody or I have shared this story with who has not ended up with a smile on his or her face. We both feel such amazement and awe at our good fortune. This experience could have gone the other direction. A great deal of credit goes to my new Weeks family for their abundance of kindness and unparalleled character.

CHAPTER 33

Collateral Damage?

I was extremely concerned that my relationship with my next-younger sister Janelle would be negatively affected by the finding of my paternal family. We are as close as any siblings can be, and we have been through a lot together. I did not and do not want her to ever feel left out of my life in any way. It is extremely important I do not ignore our relationship while growing my bonds with my new family. She has been great and supportive to me in every way possible.

My situation caused her to question her own parentage. That is unfortunate, although understandable, given my mother's tendency toward half-truths and secrecy. Janelle knows that Mom was pregnant with her when she married Moe, just as she was pregnant with Kerry when she married Sonny. Because my newly discovered father's identity was a secret for so many years, Janelle posed some tough questions to our mother about any possibility whatsoever that a different father existed for her as well.

I had serious concerns about stepping into the new sibling group and being divisive in any way. This is a wonderful family. They have been there for each other for fifty-plus years, and I am a newcomer. Nobody has said or done anything to make me think my concerns are valid. I am exceptionally thankful that there appears to be no divide. The inclusion of Melody and I has only been very heartwarmingly welcome.

Undoubtedly, there will be family members who will be in closer contact considering everyone's geographic locations, but we are in the technological world, and it will be important to keep in touch with everyone. It is a two-way street, and my new family has been great about reaching out to me just to say hello. I need to do more than just think about all my new siblings as I go about my day and need to make a better habit of communicating myself.

During a visit to Des Moines in March 2018, my sister Janelle and I had the opportunity to visit my dad's sister. Aunt Charlotte was reminiscing about meeting Janelle as a baby and meeting me for the first time when I was a toddler. She slipped and said something about Moe not being my father, and she was suddenly ashamed of letting out a secret she had kept for sixty years. I told her that I knew about everything, as did Janelle.

Aunt Charlotte still thinks that Sonny is my father, and I could see no reason to bring up the reality of Chuck Sr. being my true birth father. It is my supposition that the information would have only added embarrassment to my mother in Aunt Charlotte's view. I am content to leave it with Aunt Charlotte that I know I am not a true Vermeulen. There is no value in and would serve no purpose for her to know the actual story at this late stage.

I have stopped all activities related to finding the elusive half-brother who is reportedly a few months younger than I am. I am no longer convinced this person ever existed or that the reason my mother and Sonny split up was infidelity on Sonny's part resulting in a pregnancy with Pat Wells. I seriously question the believability of this scenario that I had heard for decades.

I do believe Pat Wells existed because my mother has always been consistent with that name, but if this child does exist, he would be no relation to me, as I am not the son of Sonny Kreider. However, he would be a sibling to my sister Kerry, and her children might choose to renew the search when and if they make their own DNA journey.

CHAPTER 34

New Family, Old Traditions

During the weekend of our very first trip to meet my new family, we were invited to come to Covington for Christmas. We learned that Chuck Sr. and Ellon had a long-standing tradition of hosting a large gathering of family and friends on Christmas Eve and wanted us to join them. The party was legendary for good food, a fun White Elephant gift exchange, and Bingo. We learned that Chuck Sr. took his bingo game very seriously. He was always the caller, and he and Ellon awarded prizes and trophies to the winners. Chuck Sr. also had no patience for anyone who shouted Bingo! if that shouter really did not have one. It sounded like a lot of fun, but we were concerned it might hurt my mother's feelings if we went to Georgia instead of Iowa for Christmas.

We received invites to come to Covington for Christmas several more times over the next few months. We really wanted to go, yet certainly did not want to upset my Des Moines family. This was the first Christmas since finding my Weeks family and our first opportunity to share in one of their longtime family traditions. We figured we had three options: stay home, drive eighteen hours each way to Iowa, or drive seven hours each way to Georgia.

We finally decided to visit Covington for just Christmas Eve and head home on Christmas Day. I told my mother about our plans two days before the trip, and she seemed to be okay with it. We are exceptionally glad we chose to drive to Georgia. Chuck and Brenda usually attended every other Christmas and had gone just the year before, but decided to attend this Christmas as well. It was such a good time, and Melody and I welcomed the opportunity to get to know nieces, nephews, and family friends a bit better.

We left for Covington the morning of December 23rd. We were literally still within a hundred yards of our own driveway when ABBA's *Dancing Queen* came on the radio. Melody and I took that as a sign that our decision to go to Georgia for Christmas Eve was the right thing to do and that we would arrive safe with Chuck Sr. as our wingman.

Cheryl's husband, John, took over the role of caller during the annual bingo game bonanza and did a fine job. Chuck, Brenda, and I all won a bingo game. (Brenda won two games!) Melody came close, but I-22 seemed to elude her repeatedly. A late-evening discussion after most guests had left revealed that maybe a total bingo ball check would be a good idea before next time as it was discovered a few were missing—the mystery of why I-22 was never called was solved.

Our decision to spend Christmas Eve with our Weeks family was another amazingly fun time. The family gatherings are just another testament to the closeness and enjoyment the family exudes when they are together. We look forward to many more of family visits and holiday fun.

MY FAMILY SHARES THEIR PERSPECTIVES

CHAPTER 35

Melody

I had watched Steve search off and on for years and years for the half-brother his mother repeatedly insisted was out there somewhere. The search was a long and involved one, and while he put it on brief pauses now and then, he never gave up on it. Thank goodness ... because the eventual outcome was so unexpected and proved to be the best anyone could ever hope to have.

In the weeks leading up to the day his mother finally (thankfully) told him the truth about who his father was, he must have run a dozen scenarios past me about the Weeks connection in his DNA results. Every scenario seemed entirely plausible, but they never panned out, and it was back to square one where he would start again. I remember clearly the day he threw out a new scenario: Maybe he was mistaken about his parentage. Maybe Sonny Kreider was not his dad. We talked about how he and Kerry resembled one another similarly enough that Sonny was likely his father and decided it must be so.

We did not know that day his suspicions would turn out to be completely correct. It was a few more weeks before his mother would finally give him the answers he needed to make it all fit together. For me, it was both a shock and a relief. Connie's long-overdue revelation suddenly made so many things finally make sense.

Nevertheless, why would she wait so long to tell Steve something that she had to know was hugely important to him? He had specifically mentioned the name Weeks to her in April, but it was July before she finally let go of the secret she had kept for sixty-one years. Why would

Steven, We Need to Talk

she wait? The answer to that question is simply because of her lifetime of living under the influence of Moe.

I always considered Moe a very likeable man, yet a very complex one. People outside his core family and friend group mostly knew the congenial, helpful, golf-loving, and hardworking Moe and had no inkling of how he could be if he became angry or irritated. Don't get me wrong; he was never anything but kind to me. While he mellowed a great deal over the years, I felt I could always sense an anger brewing just beneath the surface. I understood why keeping him on an even keel was always of the utmost importance to those closest to him.

I have no doubt that in the sixty-plus years Connie and Moe spent together that Moe absolutely believed Sonny Kreider was both Kerry's and Steve's father. I also have no doubt that, up until the day Connie finally revealed the truth to Steve about Chuck Weeks Sr., she had never breathed a word of it to another soul. This was something she confirmed for us a few months later. To divulge this secret to anyone would have been risking Moe finding out, risking judgement from friends, and risking personal embarrassment. Connie, along with everyone else in the family, had spent a lifetime avoiding angering or disappointing Moe. I think Connie and Sonny Kreider were likely the only people on the planet who knew with absolute certainty that Steve was not Sonny's child.

Based on some email exchanges between Steve and his Aunt Faith before her death a few years ago, it seemed Faith also had some very strong suspicions about who his father was not, and that was Sonny Kreider. I really do understand the reasons Connie gave for not telling Steve when Moe was alive, but he had been gone more than a year when Steve first mentioned the Weeks name to her. She should have told him right then. It is disappointing, to say the least, that she did not provide the truth until she was confronted with indisputable DNA results. She finally did, though, and for that, we are thankful.

While many details about our first meeting with this wonderful new family are a bit of a blur, I remember some parts so clearly. I was at the check-in counter in the lobby of the hotel in Conyers, Georgia, feeling a little nervous while envisioning in my head how the first meeting might play out when I heard someone off to the side quietly say, "Is that Melody?" I turned my head to see Chuck and Brenda coming toward the lobby with smiles on their faces.

Steve had just appeared in the hotel doorway with our luggage. I was trying to see Steve and Chuck meet for the first time and simultaneously check in—I did not want to miss even a single moment. Then it was my turn for hugs and I felt an immediate liking for them both. I instantly knew the rest of the weekend was going to be great.

Cheryl and Denise arrived a short time later, and we all spent probably an hour around a table in the hotel lobby before going off to dinner. I felt the same instant liking for them as I had for Chuck and Brenda. After dinner, we all spent another couple of hours around the same table back at the hotel lobby before Cheryl and Denise headed back to their parents' home around midnight.

The next day Steve and I, along with Chuck and Brenda, spent the morning roaming around the town square in Covington. We parted company after lunch in midafternoon to give everyone time to relax or nap before leaving for dinner to meet Chuck Sr., Ellon, and a few other family members. I had a few butterflies wondering how that meeting would go. Everything had gone wonderfully thus far.

We knew Chuck Sr. had spent the previous month trying to reconcile and get comfortable with the news that he had a son he had never known about. He had concerns that this revelation might somehow diminish his reputation or cause people to lose respect for him. His reputation and honor were extremely important to him, and once he realized everyone he and Ellon told about Steve were happy and excited for him, he knew his worries were unfounded.

We went to the restaurant with Chuck and Brenda in their car. Chuck was backing into a parking space off to the side when a car drove by and Chuck said, "There they are." I took a deep breath and crossed my fingers in hopes that everything was going to go as well as I thought it would. I could see Denise and Cheryl with their dad waiting at the curb. Cheryl spotted us coming across the parking lot. She said something to her dad, and I saw him look toward us and smile. *Whew!* Things were going to be fine, I could just feel it! Chuck Sr. and Steve shook hands and spoke a few words at the curb, and then we all headed inside.

We followed the hostess to the room where we sat for dinner, and I saw Ellon standing with someone. (I cannot remember who because my eyes were only on Ellon, and I had the fleeting thought, "I hope she likes us.") I went up to her and put out my hand to introduce myself, but she went for the hug (which suited me just fine) and called me "sweetie."

I took the chair next to hers, and she turned toward me and said, "You're so pretty."

I literally had to take a deep breath and try very hard not to cry at how incredibly kind and sweet and gracious she was. Would all spouses and family members be this welcoming to a sixty-one-year-old "child" if he suddenly were to appear out of nowhere as Steve had? If not, they should take a lesson out of Ellon's book about how to be accepting and understanding in a situation such as this.

It is still amazing to me how warm and welcoming and genuinely nice this entire family is from the parents all the way down to their grandchildren and great-grandchildren. All these months later, I still get misty-eyed when I reflect on that night. Being around this family is always so comfortable, so much fun … It feels so much like home.

CHAPTER 36

Janelle

When Steven asked me for my perspective, my immediate thought was a flashback to conversations I had with Mom when her long-held secret broke open. Mom and her sister, Faith, were quite active around the Air Force base on Cape Cod during their teens and early adulthood. None of the activities were harmful, just young women seeking entertainment such as attending dances and meeting a host of young men from various areas of the country.

Mom had told us many times that she and her family did not grow up under the best of circumstances. She had moved to Cape Cod as a baby, and her early life had been tough. Her father had left the family home when she was just seven years old, leaving Mimi with four children and precious little of anything else. Work for Mimi became an overwhelming force as she struggled to care for her four children. This was the beginning of what Mom always referred to as a loveless home. Mimi was always working, which left the children to grow up on their own. As they got older (in order of birth—Faith, Mom, Donnie, and Sandra), the children began exploring other avenues for the attention they were not getting at home. As the saying goes, even bad attention was better than no attention.

When Mom was in her early teens, Mimi had married a wonderful man named Walter. (I only knew him as Grandpa.) Mimi started a carryout pizza restaurant that she spent many, many hours operating. Walter spent countless hours assisting her with managing the restaurant and holding down a full-time job with the local school system after his retirement from the Merchant Marines. The attention paid to the children did not improve, as Mom recalled. If anything, they gained even more independence because both her mother and step-father were very busy with work and life and had little time for the four children.

I should also mention that per Mom's recollections, there was significant alcoholic behavior exhibited by most of the adults surrounding Mom and her siblings. When their parents were not at the restaurant, they were overindulging with adult beverages to cope with their exhaustion from their long hours of work.

As Mom developed into a young woman, male attention toward her grew—and she liked it. It filled a void she felt because of the lack of attention and guidance in her home life. The same may also have applied to her sisters. The local Air Force base provided the recreational activities of drinking and dancing as well as a semi captive audience of young men who were ever too eager to date young women.

On Cape Cod, there is an on and an off season for shore and beach activities. The Air Force base provided year-round entertainment. In her late teen years, Mom, and occasionally Faith (who was two years older than Mom), would spend nearly every weekend evening hanging out at the base, waiting for the fun to begin. They were seldom waiting long for an invite into the enlisted men's club, and they were inside for a night of dancing and drinking. Yes, they were underage for drinking, but that was never a problem. Things were much different in those days, and everyone looked the other way if the airmen were having a good time.

As is often the case when you mix young women, young men, alcohol, and hormones, the inevitable get-togethers happened. There may have been some precautions taken, but it was mostly dumb luck if pregnancies did not result. It was a time when couples "did the right thing" when girls got into trouble. This is how Mom came to marry Sonny Kreider. She was in trouble, so to speak, with Kerry, after dating Sonny for a while, and the right thing happened soon after she disclosed her pregnancy to him. Sonny did not really want to be married and left the marriage very soon after the ceremony occurred. Mom even stated Sonny did not spend their wedding night with her. Her marriage to Sonny was virtually over from the start. It was just a few weeks after Kerry was born when Mom started going to the Air Force base again for evenings of fun and entertainment.

The same activities generally lead to the same outcomes, and soon she became pregnant with Steven. This circumstance was different, however, because the father was not going to be able to "do the right thing" because she was still married—albeit separated—to Sonny Kreider. She had to pass Steven off as Sonny's child due to the Massachusetts laws of that time. The legally married husband's name went on the birth certificate as the father, regardless of who the biological father was. After Steven was born, Mom took some time off from visiting the Air Force base and began raising her two babies.

Citing abandonment, she divorced Sonny about a year later and began dating when she could arrange a night out. As usual, the Air Force base was the logical and closest entertainment place to go for a fun time, and back she went to enjoy her evenings. It was in late 1956 when she met and began dating Moe, my father. After a few months, she was in trouble again, this time with me, and they were married shortly thereafter. They were together almost sixty years before his passing.

Mom grew up always seeking love and acceptance, which she found in abundance with the young men stationed at the Air Force base. While this may not have always been the proper love and attention we might understand, at the time it was what she determined was best for her. By her own admissions, she experienced many great times during those years. She endured many negative situations, too.

Mom was always a rebel in many ways. She rebelled against the lack of love and attention at home by chasing love (or her interpretation of what love was) wherever she could find it. She rebelled against the stereotypes of proper young women at the time, as she was more than willing to be involved with her dates. She rebelled against the necessity of being a stay-at-home single parent and continued trying to better her situation and find a life partner. She had a rebel mentality through her final days; nobody was going to tell her how to think, what to do, or how to behave. *Period.*

I am happy that Steven has found such a wonderful new family through his DNA search. I have told him that because the Weeks family is important to him, they are important to me. Steven is my family; therefore, the Weeks's are now my family. I look forward to meeting them and hope they look forward to meeting me. This will be quite the new adventure for us all.

CHAPTER 37

Ellon

I answered a phone call on a Sunday afternoon from a man requesting to speak with Charles Weeks. I handed the phone to Chuck and headed off to take nap. Chuck did not mention anything about the call later that evening, and I presumed it was a call for his business, Weeks Investigative Services, or related to his duties with the VFW. There was no indication of the life-changing news that he would tell me the next day.

As Chuck was driving me to an eye doctor appointment the following morning, he started a conversation with "Ellon Louise," and I knew that something important was about to come. He said, "Ellon Louise, I have something to tell you, and I don't know how to tell you." He went on to explain, "A man called last night and said he is my son!" It was like a hammer had hit me right in the forehead. I was in disbelief. Right out of the blue, as they say. I asked him what he was going to do about it, and he seemed to think he would not hear any more about it. He was certainly not going to tell the children or his friends about the call. Little did we know that by the time Chuck had told me about the call, all our children had already learned of Steve and were completely thrilled with the knowledge of having a new brother.

Denise and Cheryl came over the next day and we began talking about their call and what they had learned about Steve. I, of course, told them of Chuck's call and their father telling me during our car ride to my doctor visit about the conversation between him and Steve. They showed me a picture they found on his social media page, and

I was shocked. He looked just like Chuck's brother, Philip Weeks. Chuck walked into the family room at that time, and when the girls asked him to come over to the table and see a picture of Steve, he replied he did not want to see it. Denise, in her infinite wisdom, said to Chuck, "Dad, don't you be mean to him. He has done nothing wrong and neither have you. You did not know he existed before the phone call."

Chuck then turned to me and said, "I leave it up to you," meaning I would be the one to decide whether we pursued this new relationship.

I quickly told Chuck that this would be entirely his decision. Because we had told him that Steve looked just like his brother Philip, Chuck went directly to the phone and called his brother to share the news. Once he had finished that call, he began to tell all our friends.

We had plans to meet Steve and Melody for dinner the first weekend of August. We hugged upon meeting that first time, and I just fell in love with them both. Now I cannot imagine life without them.

CHAPTER 38

Denise

I had just gotten into my car for the long commute home late on a Sunday evening. I worked a job that required me to stay near my work location five or six days each week. I drove an hour and forty minutes home for a couple of days and then repeated the drive to return for the next week of work. While sitting in my car preparing to leave and setting my phone up so I could listen to a popular radio podcast, I decided to check my private social media messages. I saw an intriguing message from some stranger asking if I knew Charles Weeks, born in 1936.

I'm the kind of person who trusts most people up front. I know you are not supposed to disclose private information to people you don't know, but I did in this instance. I immediately responded to the question, "Yes, that's my father," and then followed up with something like, "How are you connected?"

The other person responded that it would be easier to explain if we talked on the phone. Facing a long drive, I thought, "*What the hell. I'll call him*". While I was pulling out of the parking lot onto the main road, I dialed the number he had given me and was turning onto the interstate when he answered. I said hello and asked him how we were connected. After a couple of sentences of explanation, he said, "I'm your brother," and that is how my story with Steve Vermeulen began.

My father did not have a lot of family we knew as we grew up. We knew his brother Philip and his wife, Joyce, and their four daughters, although not well. We had never lived near them and had not visited them since we were small children, but my parents talked to them regularly by phone. I knew my dad had an aunt named Augusta (Aunt Gussie to us), who was quite aged and has now passed, but that was really all the family we knew from our paternal side. I suspected there were others we were related to and had never met; however, I had not thought much on the subject over the years.

When I saw Steve's message, I thought maybe we had a chance to connect with a long-lost cousin or the like. How exciting! However, never in a million years did I expect him to say he was my brother.

To me, my parents are the epitome of virtue. They met on a blind date, fell in love, and married a month later. I always believed they were the only two people in each other's lives. It hard to imagine your parents with anyone else when they have been together for fifty-eight years. I know they both had prior boyfriends and girlfriends, but certainly no one that they would have been intimate with. Why, that's just crazy talk! But now someone was suggesting my dad had another son and I had another brother? How did this happen ... and when?

As I remember it, Steve began his story by explaining that my dad was nineteen years old at the time. My immediate thought was, Yep, I raised a couple of nineteen-year-old boys, and that explains it. Then I remembered my parents had met and married when they were both twenty-four, so it could not have happened when they knew each other.

Following a whole lot of "oh my Gods" from me, Steve said, "My mom was separated from my dad at the time, and my mom never told your dad that he had a son." Yep, it all makes sense now, I thought. Because I knew my dad had not cheated on my mom during their marriage, I was all right.

We talked for quite a while. I was not upset. I was not jealous. I was not mad ... yet. I was truly interested. The thought did cross my mind that Steve may have ulterior motives, but that was just a passing thought. He and I talked comfortably about the information he had compiled until I realized I had a piece of information—a jolting piece of information—that the rest of my siblings did not have. *OMG!*

I said to Steve, "I'm sorry, but I have got to get off this phone and call my sisters. We'll talk again soon." This information was just too explosive to keep to myself. It never occurred to me to keep it a secret. That is just not how things worked in our tight-knit sibling circle. I could not possibly hold onto this information that my sisters and brother did not have.

It was not that I wanted to get anyone in trouble or be a tattletale; we just do not keep things from each other that are this important. Our military lifestyle growing up created a fierce bond between my four siblings and myself. Quite frankly, this news was just too big to hold onto by myself.

Knowing two of my sisters, Cheryl and Debra, were on vacation together in Florida, I immediately called Cheryl's cell phone. When she answered, I said, "Get Debra and go somewhere where no one can hear you." I waited a minute while she got my sister, went into a bedroom, and shut the door away from their children and grandchildren.

Now, if you live the kind of quiet lifestyle my siblings and I live, you can imagine being the one with news that the others do not have. Up to this point, our explosive news would be something like I found a Coach purse at Goodwill for $10! or Granny asked me to come over to her house just to get something out from under her bed! It is rare to possess life-altering news in our family. We are all law-abiding, hardworking people who are good friends, good employees, and good neighbors. I am the only one who has had much of any drama at all in life, and that is only due to my multiple marriages.

My one and only concern up to this point was my mom. We needed to make sure we did not let Mom find out unless Dad told her himself. I knew Steve had talked to my dad, and my dad was gracious—not even attempting to deny his brief fling with Steve's mother.

I took a short breath and blurted it out. "I got a phone call from a guy named Steve ..." I then proceeded to tell them everything I knew.

Cheryl said, "No *way*!" in the way she always says it, with strong emphasis on *way*. Debra, too. The three of us talked back and forth about the what-ifs.

At the end of the conversation—when it had sunk in that we were now six, not five—I asked Cheryl to contact Chuck and Janel, and we hung up. No one acted or verbalized anything negative.

The next day I found myself at my parents' house. I stole a look at my dad, knowing he had already talked to Steve. He seemed the exact same as any other day. I talked to my mom. Everything was as it always was. I wondered if Mom knew and was just not saying anything.

My thoughts at the time were beginning to really expand on what I had learned. I began thinking about how Steve's mom had deceived him and about how she had deceived my dad, my sisters, my brother, and me. That is when my agitation about the deception began to grow.

The next day, I was at my parents' house again. I do not remember how the subject came up, but Dad expressed his knowledge of Steve and so did Mom. My mom said, "Why didn't you say anything?" I said, "I didn't know if Dad wanted you to know!"

We began talking about the circumstances of Steve's existence. We talked about how everyone felt when they found out. Dad found out we all knew about Steve and was not especially happy. He had decided not to tell anyone but my mom. Oops! Too late for that!

My dad was slightly angry as well. *No!* He was not meeting Steve or even talking to him again. He said he was a nice enough person, but he had no plans to have a relationship with him. I know my dad was embarrassed that his children, who he knew revered him so much, had found out he possessed human frailties and weaknesses like the rest of humanity.

I remember being thirteen years old and learning about the human baby gestation period. I counted the days between my parents' wedding date and my birthday. It came up a few days short. I was not a premature birth as far as I knew, and I thought I had discovered my parents had had relations before their wedding. I made this observation to my dad. I do not recall the exact words he used, but I do remember he was not amused.

As I left my parents' house that day, I stood nose-to-nose with my dad and said with my finger pointed in his face (which, I might add, is not a safe posture to take with the elder Charles), "Don't you be mean to him! He didn't do anything wrong and neither did you!" With that, I left.

From my mom's recount, that statement changed my dad's thinking. He tried to put the decision to have a friendship with Steve on my mom, but she would not let him. She told him it was his decision, and soon he decided to meet Steve.

We met for the first time at the hotel in Covington and visited for a bit before heading to a restaurant for dinner. Yes, Steve looked like our family. He displayed many of the same mannerisms as my dad, to the point of being uncanny. His wife, Melody, is a delight and the more playful side of their union. I bonded with them both immediately.

I have never felt weird about having a new brother Steve. I have no issue with him now being the oldest. Being the oldest was a burden growing up, and I would not wish it on my worst enemy. For example, this is how Charles Weeks taught me to drive a car:

He spent fifty hours yelling at me while I practiced driving with him. I know now how frightened he was that one of his children was going to be driving, but at the time, I thought he was a giant idiot. I am sure the thought of doubling his car insurance was at the forefront of his mind, too.

While standing outside of the vehicle, he got a ruler and measured how many inches I rolled back on a steep hill from a complete stop in a 1965 Volkswagen with manual transmission—repeatedly.

I had to read a textbook from the Highway Patrol called *Highway Homicide*. I then had to write a report on it and give it to my dad to be graded. I also had to pass an oral exam administered by my dad on the same textbook. Get the picture?

In comparison, by the time Debra was ready to take the test for her driver's license, I explained to her how to drive while I laid in bed, and then she taught herself while driving back and forth in front of our house. I am not sure my parents even knew that daughters three and four even got their driver's licenses. After watching what I had to go through, Cheryl elected to get her license at twenty-one years old, and Mom taught her.

It is funny to tell that story now, but what is not funny is how Steve's mother deceived him, her family, and our family. The more I get to know Steve and Melody, the more fortunate I feel as a person. When he and Melody talk to me on the phone, they have a knack for making me feel like I am the most important person in their lives. I am sure they do that for others as well.

Unlike some of my siblings, I do not recall many of the specifics of the phone conversations or the multiple meetings with Steve and Melody. It has been easy, fun, and fulfilling.

I am sorry that Steve did not know us when we were young, and I am sorry we did not know him. We had a strict upbringing, but we had a lot of fun together, which he, I am sure, would have delighted in, too.

I am lucky. I never felt as if I had something that was not quite right the way Steve has told us he felt. I have terrific siblings who support me in all aspects, and that is hard to come by. Steve had the love and support of his siblings who I hope to meet someday soon.

I possess an intense dislike for the deception that Steve's mother perpetuated on not just Steve, but all of us. She robbed my dad of knowing his son. She robbed me and my siblings of knowing Steve and growing up with our brother in our lives. We almost missed knowing him at all. He was here our entire lives, and we did not know. How sad is that?

Without his DNA discovery, we would all be still none the wiser, and his mother would have taken the truth about his parentage and our story to her grave. None of us deserved that. Her pride impacted so many—our children ... our grandchildren. How selfish she was!

As it was, my dad and Steve almost missed each other completely. It was a sad day when my dad passed away in August 2017 after having only known of Steve for two months and having only met him three weeks earlier. Thankfully, though, they met and talked, and each was happy to finally know the other. Neither dwelled on what they had missed; they were just pleased that they knew they belonged to each other.

For those reading this story and keeping a secret like this, *please* understand that your decision to tell someone about his or her true heritage, or possible heritage, profoundly impacts that person as well as countless other individuals. There are always consequences to behavior, and sometimes the results of that behavior have irreversible consequences. We do not dwell on the past that we lost with Steve, but we look forward to the many years and memories in the future!

CHAPTER 39

Chuck

Call me Charlie.

It was warm summer day in early July 2017 that I received a call that would change my life. It was during the early morning hours as I sat at my desk. The office was eerily quiet when the sound of a phone ringing startled me. As I quickly located the phone, I noticed my sister's name in the display. My only thought: *Oh my God! Who died?* Sorry, I digress.

My birth name is Charles Edward Weeks Jr., but I have used the nickname Chuck since my teenage years. I was the second child born to Charles Edward Weeks and Ellon Louise Driver. I have four beautiful sisters (in age order: Denise, Cheryl, Debra, and Janel) whom I love and adore with all my heart. We are all about a year apart except for our youngest sister, Janel. I believe she was an accidental blessing nine months after our parents rendezvoused in Hawaii during the Vietnam Conflict.

My father was an officer in the US Army for most of our childhood. My loving mother was the dutiful officer's wife and our primary caregiver. Like many families of that era, our father controlled the household and was a strict disciplinarian. My sisters and I were always under his watchful eye and were expected to behave like little soldiers. We were well trained in our respective roles, but when we failed, it was usually met with harsh discipline.

As a military family, we moved frequently and had to leave friends behind. Each one of us became proficient at making new friends and adapting to our new environment. These abilities followed us into adulthood. They are some of the reasons that we can quickly adapt to unfamiliar situations and accept new people in our lives. However, for our protection and sanctuary, my sisters and I also developed a fierce sense of loyalty to each other. This meant that we would collectively close ranks on our common enemies or anyone we perceived as a threat, which has included our father. I believe our father unwittingly instilled and cultivated this virtue in all of us.

As with most children of our generation, shortly after we attained the age of freedom, we moved from the family home to begin new lives and start our own families. Through the years, my sisters and I relocated to various parts of the country, but eventually, we all returned to the East Coast (except for Janel, who still lives in Kansas). During those years, my siblings and I always remained close and visited each other as often as possible. I made my home in Virginia and married the love of my life, Brenda.

For the first fifty-five years of my life, I have been the only son of Charles Weeks. My claim to fame (which I often bragged about to anyone who would listen) was being the only male heir to the Weeks family name. I apologize for the jealously that some of you are now feeling. I also regularly boasted about being the only male child in a family with four sisters, which I claimed gave me special insight into the mind of the opposite sex. However, as I have matured in life, I have learned that this was a complete fallacy—a fact that is frequently reinforced by my loving wife, Brenda.

Now I will disclose a secret that I have held close to my heart—a secret that I never shared with anyone until July 10, 2017. My secret is that I always wanted a brother—a male sibling who understood me better than any other person did, a brother who would share an unbreakable union no matter where we wandered or what life offered us. I know this sounds a bit melodramatic, and realistically, we probably would have argued, fought, and hated each other from time to time, but I still wanted a brother.

As I journeyed through life, these feelings waned, but never disappeared. I am reminded of what I missed each time we visit my sisters and sisters-in-law. They exhibit a special bond that I believe is unique to same-sex siblings (like twins). A special connection that comes from shared DNA, experiences, and spending a lifetime together. Don't get me wrong, I believe brothers and sisters can also have a unique bond, just not the same type of relationship that same-sex siblings share. Now that I have gotten that out of my system and stopped feeling sorry for myself, let me continue my story.

The date was July 10, 2017, a day that will hold special meaning to me for the rest of my life. By all standards, it started out as an ordinary day that turned extraordinary. After arriving at work, I began my daily routine, which was interrupted by a phone call from my sister, Cheryl. She began spinning this unbelievable tale that began sixty-two years ago in New England and ended with me having a brother. My initial thought was, "*Wait. What did she just say?*" And then my head exploded.

Let me explain: When Cheryl called that morning, she informed me that a man named Steve Vermeulen had contacted our father and claimed he might be his son. She went on to say that Steve's mother and our father had an affair when Dad was about nineteen years old. Cheryl explained that our father had never been told about the pregnancy or that he might have a son. Cheryl added that Steve had tried to contact all of us and had recently sent private messages. (Unfortunately, I never check my social media messages.) The rest of her words were a blur as my mind jumped between "Oh my god, I have a brother!" and "How the hell could I have a brother?"

To say that I was excited about the idea of having a brother might have been a bit of an understatement, but my joy was clouded with suspicion. My cynical side kept reminding me that things like this only happen on *Jerry Springer*. However, while my skeptical brain wrestled with the thought of whether this was real, my heart was open to the possibility.

The thought of having an unknown brother for so many years perplexed me because I trusted my father. How could he not have known that he had another son? Why wouldn't the woman have told him about the pregnancy? I wanted to believe that my father would never have kept something like this from his family. I also knew that he would have been a presence in Steve's life, especially because he had always wanted another son—hence, the reason my parents had three more girls before they raised the white flag.

So, I did what any rational person would do: I became a social media stalker. (For legal reasons, I will refer to this as the *investigation*.) The investigation began with my social media account to see if Steve had really sent me a message. When I found a message from Steve Vermeulen, I carefully read and weighed the value of each word. (Sadly, I really did this.) My conclusion was that Steve seemed sincere, and he was trying to contact a possible family member ... Or was this really just a scam?

My next investigative step was to examine Steve's social media profile. When I opened his page, it appeared to be normal with no immediate red flags. I began scrolling through the various photographs that contained many unknown faces until the moment I saw *the photo*. I vividly recall *the photo* because it appeared to be a picture of my Uncle Philip (albeit a younger, handsomer version—you're welcome, Steve) holding a baby. I later learned that the baby was Steve's grandson and my new great-nephew.

In that instant, I knew the man depicted in the photograph had to share the Weeks DNA. A wave of emotion enveloped me as I realized that Steve was a member of our family. It was hard to process all the new information that began running through my head, such as: I have five siblings, Steve is the oldest child, I am a middle child, I am no longer the only male, and, most importantly, *holy crap, I have a brother*!

I downloaded Steve's photo and put it side-by-side with a recent photograph of our Uncle Philip, which I sent to all the sisters, my wife, and my sons. They all seemed to agree that Steve had an uncanny resemblance to Uncle Philip, and most of us could see physical traits from our father. At that moment, one thing that we all agreed upon was that Steve had to be our brother.

That night I called Cheryl to get more information about Steve's phone call. Cheryl explained that Steve had provided some details about the relationship between his mother and our father when they were both nineteen years old. Apparently, Dad admitted to a brief affair with Steve's mother while he was in the Air Force but had no idea that it had resulted in a pregnancy. Steve acknowledged that his mother never disclosed that information to him, and he had been raised with the belief that his biological father was a different man. Steve had never heard the name Weeks until he submitted a DNA sample for testing.

After hanging up, I could not wait to call my brother. How strange it sounded to say, *"my brother"* and know it was true. I also realized that my fifty-five years of waiting for that damn stork to deliver me a brother was finally over. Don't get me wrong, I delayed making the call for about an hour—but who wouldn't be a little apprehensive and nervous with all the unknowns? Would he like me? Would I like him? Was he married? Did he have children? Where did he work? Where did he live?

When I finally made the call, I could feel my heart pounding (that is always a good sign at my age) as the phone began to ring. When I heard a male voice answer Hello? I strangely knew it was my brother's voice. Well, it really was not that strange because I called his cell number. I can honestly say that when the realization hit me that I was talking to my brother, emotion overcame me. After all, I had long since given up hope of ever having a brother.

We talked like long-lost friends for about thirty minutes, discussing things that most brothers already knew about each other, such as families and jobs. We also began planning a face-to-face meeting as soon as possible. The only uncomfortable moments for me (which were self-inflicted) were when I kept using the phrase "my father" instead of "our father." I was concerned that Steve might perceive this as an insult. I know some of you might say that it was a Freudian slip, but it was just a conditioned response that I had to relearn. In truth, Steve had me at hello.

Steve also gave me some insight into his journey to find his father. As I discovered from later conversations, his search was much more involved than I originally thought. It was my understanding that his journey began, oddly enough, when he was enlisting in the Air Force at nineteen years old and continued for the next forty-two years.

I will never understand the emotional journey that my brother traveled when he discovered that his dad was not his biological father or that he might have another sibling…all the moments along the way when his triumphant discoveries ended in bitter disappointment. I also wonder how Steve felt when he realized that the search was over. I only hope that what he learned has been worth all his sacrifices. I know that his sacrifices gave me one of the greatest moments of my life, and I look forward to our new chapter.

I am still amazed and impressed with the perseverance and determination that my big brother showed during the search for his biological father. So, I just want to take a moment and say thank you to Steve for his commitment, strength of character, and ingenuity in finding the ultimate truth. I am especially thankful because if Steve had ever given up, I would have never met my brother. I also wanted to give special thanks to my sister-in-law, Melody, who I know was a constant source of support for Steve and suffered many of his highs and lows with him. All right, that's enough sappy stuff for now—let's get back to the story.

The next few days were a whirlwind, filled with multiple conversations between my wife, sons, sisters, parents, and friends. We were all amazed and thrilled at what we had just gained. Every member of the family viewed the new additions in a very positive light. I can honestly say that there was not one negative comment that I heard from any family member or friend. And yes, I told this story to anyone who would listen and even a few people I'm sure wanted me to shut up. Everyone seemed happy for us, and we were all anxious to meet Steve and Melody.

However, I do know our father had some reservations. It became known that after his initial conversation with Steve, our dad thought about hiding this information from his family. The thought that my father believed this was an option is hilarious because before he had even ended that phone call with Steve, my sisters and I were already making plans to meet our new brother and sister-in-law.

Because the proverbial cat was out of the bag, my father had no choice but to acknowledge that Steve existed. I am sure it was a very uncomfortable conversation when he shared this information with his wife of fifty-seven years, even though this relationship had occurred several years before my parents ever met.

By our standards today, events like this are common and should be celebrated, especially because a child would have no fault in these situations. But, by the standards of our parents' generation, this was not something that was quickly accepted or even talked about. This would have been a secret that many people would have hidden from public scrutiny. Just for the record, I am not making excuses for my father's initial reaction to this situation, but if he had continued with his refusal to acknowledge Steve, it would have caused irreparable damage to the respect I have for him.

Just as a side note, our father was a very proud and stubborn man. He had built himself up from virtually nothing, so his name and reputation meant almost everything to him. The only thing that meant more to our father was his family, and we all dearly loved him for that. I believe that the initial shock of learning about Steve embarrassed my father and, in his eyes, exposed him as an imperfect man. Trust me, my father was one of the greatest men I have ever known, but he had his flaws. (Thank goodness I didn't inherit any.)

Despite all his earlier reservations, our father saw the error of his ways and completely accepted Steve and Melody into the family. I believe my mother and sisters had a lot to do with this change of heart. My dad even began telling his family and friends about his new son, Steve.

By late July 2017, Steve and I were finally making definitive plans to meet in Georgia for the first time. We decided on Conyers, Georgia, because it seemed like the best location to meet most of the family at one time. We discussed two dates in either August or September and settled on the first weekend of August. Although it was short notice, we felt that because our dad was not getting any younger, sooner was better than later. We would later learn that this decision was either divine intervention or incredible forethought, depending on your belief.

On August 4, 2017, Brenda and I arrived early at the hotel in Conyers. We had been selected by the family as liaisons for Steve and Melody's visit. I waited anxiously for several hours before Steve and Melody finally arrived at the hotel. They were a little later than expected because of significant traffic delays. When Steve called to inform me they were in the lobby, my anxiety level escalated, and I became uncharacteristically hesitant. I recall asking Brenda, "Should we go to the lobby now, or should we just wait until later?" Luckily, Brenda was quick to answer with an affirmative, "Now."

As we walked toward the lobby, the anticipation of meeting my brother heightened with every step. I also remember how clouded my thinking became, as it was dominated by only one thought: Should I hug Steve or just shake his hand? As trivial as that may sound, I was literally meeting a stranger, and I did not how Steve would react to the intimacy of a hug. When we finally made it the lobby, I immediately spied a familiar face from my social media investigation and knew it had to be my brother.

Steve was familiar in a way that's hard for me to describe, but it felt like he was someone I had known my whole life but had not seen in a really, really, long time—and he really did resemble Uncle Philip.

I remember the moment when Steve and I finally greeted each other and shared our first awkward hug. Yes, I went for the hug because I wanted Steve to know how happy I was to meet him. I also hugged my sister-in-law, Melody, who seemed like a warm and loving person. That turned out to be a gross understatement because Melody is an incredible person. Our warm greetings gave way to some general pleasantries and conversation before we departed for our rooms to freshen up before dinner.

Of course, I immediately phoned Cheryl and Denise to inform them that Steve and Melody had arrived. They had planned to come to the hotel to meet our brother and sister-in-law before dinner. When our sisters arrived, we all met back in the lobby. My sisters exchanged hugs and hellos with Steve and Melody before we all sat down for some conversation before dinner. I think we were all a little dumbstruck as we looked across the table at each other and began our first face-to-face family conversation.

We soon traveled to the restaurant and continued getting to know each other. I must tell you about one jaw-dropping moment when Steve said something that quelled any doubts (I didn't have any) about his paternal bloodline. I do not recall what he was referencing at the time, but Steve used the phrase "shit for brains." Now I have heard this phrase used numerous times in my fifty-five years of life, as I was frequently the reason for its use, but I have never heard another person use this phrase except for our father.

We were all blown away as we discussed the likelihood that Steve's use of that phrase was simply a coincidence. That expression, along with other phrases, quirks (Steve and our father frequently sweep the top of the table with their hand), and similar food preferences (eating canned spinach soaked with vinegar) that Steve shares with our father has made me feel an even closer connection.

On Saturday evening, Steve finally got to meet his father for the first time. I will not go into detail about this meeting because I intentionally tried to fade into the background. I understood that this was a very personal moment for Steve and it should be his alone to experience. It suffices to say that the remainder of that evening seemed to go very well. Just a side note: I have rarely seen the kind of joy on our father's face that I saw that evening when he met his oldest son for the first time. It is a vision and memory I will cherish forever.

The time seemed to fly by, and on Sunday morning, Steve and Melody returned to North Carolina. As I reflected on the weekend, I was elated at how well it had gone. I was able to learn a lot about my big brother and felt like we had started to develop a brotherly bond. Brenda and I also learned how much we really liked both Steve and Melody. I was already looking forward to our future adventures together.

I regret that I must end my story on such a sad note, but on August 28, 2017, our father, Charles Weeks Sr. passed away. I remember calling Steve to give him the news. I don't know how Steve felt when he heard that our father had passed away because he had just recently met him. I would never ask that question, and a positive or negative response wouldn't change my feelings about Steve—especially since Steve had recently lost the man he had known as Dad for sixty years and was still grieving that loss when our father passed.

I will say this about Steve: when I gave him the news about our father, he was compassionate and understanding. He immediately offered his support and assistance with anything that was needed. That's exactly what I would have expected from my brother.

The next time we saw Steve and Melody was at our father's funeral. I am not going to elaborate on the funeral because I don't want to detract from Steve's amazing journey to find his father. Let's just say that I am extremely thankful that Steve and Dad had a chance to meet and that he and Melody are now a part of our lives. However, I do wish he'd had a little more time to get to know the man I called my dad.

The soldier, above all other people, prays for peace, for he must suffer and bear the deepest wounds and scars of war.

—Douglas MacArthur, American soldier

Rest in peace, Dad.

CHAPTER 40

Cheryl

Let me start by giving you some background on our family. I was raised as a military brat in a very close-knit family. That's not to say we were a picture-perfect family—far from it—but my sisters and brother were the closest friends I had, and they still are. There was Denise (the oldest), Charles Jr. (the only boy), me (the middle child), Debra (the quiet one), and Janel (the baby of the family). We were all very close in age and spent a lot of time together. We fussed and fought like all siblings, and then we made up and went along together.

Our parents, Charles Sr. and Ellon, were, we thought, normal parents. Dad was very difficult to live with at times, and we spent a fair amount of time wishing he would just go away. Mom, on the other hand, was our rock, our shoulder to cry on, and our protection when needed.

Our childhood was not perfect, but we all made it out together, and I lived to tell the tale. I am not sure I can adequately express how I feel about my siblings. They have seen me through the best and worst times of my life, and I would take a bullet for any one of them. I once had a coworker ask me if I ever went on vacation to see friends, not just family. I had to explain that my siblings *ARE* my friends. I cannot imagine going on vacation without them.

So many, many years later in July 2017, Debra and I were on our yearly vacation to St. Augustine, Florida, with our families when I received a call from our sister, Denise. She said I needed to get Debra, go to a private space, and put her on speakerphone. Once I did this, she proceeded to drop a bomb on us. She told us she had just gotten off the phone with a man by the name of Steve who is our *brother*! *What?!*

Deb and I were absolutely speechless. She started telling us the story that Steve had relayed to her about how he had spent his childhood, how he had found out about the connection to us, and that he had already talked to our dad. While she was telling us this, I grabbed my iPad and started searching for him on social media. When I finally got his name right and found his page, I looked at his picture. *Holy shit!* He looked like Uncle Philip, our dad's younger brother. I immediately showed Debra who said the same thing. Then I had Denise look him up too. Same conclusion.

We talked about this for a little while longer. Should we say anything to Dad or wait for him to bring it up, about how shocked he must be, wondering if Mom knew, and about how this would affect the whole family. So many thoughts were running through our heads. Denise said she was not going to say anything to our parents right away, but she told me to call our brother Chuck and our sister Janel and tell them. I called them both, and the result was the same—absolute amazement and curiosity about this new brother. There was, of course, concern that he was a nutcase trying to swindle our parents in some way, so our brother was given the task of checking up on him to make sure this was legit. Luckily, we did not find any negative information about him. He didn't have a criminal record or have any shady information about him on the internet. I shared the picture of Steve I had gotten from his social media page, and everyone agreed about him looking like one of us.

Hearing the story about how he found out about our father was, to say the least, very upsetting. I knew, without a shred of doubt, that Dad never knew anything about him. I know our father, and I know how important family is to him. He would never have walked away from his child. It broke my heart to know Dad had been robbed of knowing his firstborn child and never getting to see him or know him, and we were robbed of knowing our big brother. Dad made a comment well after he had talked to Steve that he would never be able to make up that lost time to him. I felt like Steve's mother, in keeping this from him, robbed all of us, and I really hate that it made Dad feel like he failed Steve in some way. I try to understand the reasons behind it, but I still feel cheated.

I feel like our brother, Chuck, had been cheated even more. Things with Dad might have been easier for him if he had not been the only son. It could not have been easy on Chuck being raised with nothing but sisters around. He has always been the best big brother in the world, but I am sure he would have loved having a male sibling who understood him better than a sister ever could. Maybe things would not have been so hard for Denise if she had not been the oldest and had a buffer between her and Dad, but that is all water under the bridge now.

Now we had to find out more about our new brother. I was concerned about my dad's feelings now that he knew, and how he would feel about all of us knowing, too. We still did not know if Mom knew. Because we did know all of this happened years before Mom and Dad met, it wasn't a case of having to come to grips with infidelity. It was simply a situation that involved a nineteen-year-old boy and a girl with a little too much experience and not enough birth control. All my siblings except one have raised boys, and we all know how they think. None of us felt Dad had done anything wrong. Steve had not done anything wrong. It was just the way life goes sometimes.

Several days later a group conference call was set up to give us all a chance to speak and start getting to know everyone. It would also give all of us the opportunity to hear the story straight from Steve, so he didn't have to retell the story five more times. All of us had our spouses on the call with us, and as is the norm with us, we were all talking at the same time, firing questions off to Steve and Melody (his wife), laughing, and cutting up with each other; just really having a good talk.

We discovered Steve had one son and a grandson. We marveled over the fact that we had so many family names in common and how often Steve would use phrases that sounded like they came from Dad's mouth. They were so patient answering all our questions, and they both have a wonderful sense of humor. I do not know how much got accomplished that first hour and a half, but I know there was never any awkwardness or lag in the conversation. It just felt right. At the end of the conversation, we were all making plans to meet in person.

At this point, we weren't sure if Dad would be agreeable to meeting Steve in person, but we were determined to do it anyway. We all continued talking with Dad and Mom about the situation over the coming days. As Dad got more comfortable with it, he began telling the important people in his life. His brother, then Mom's siblings, and then his circle of very close friends. All of them were very supportive.

I will be forever thankful to them for that, as it made my dad so happy. He had always been very concerned about his reputation within his group, and I know he was concerned they would think less of him. They did not. And, thankfully, after Mom got through the shock of it, she became curious about Steve and was looking forward to meeting him.

It came time to meet in person. Chuck and Brenda met Steve and Melody first at the hotel where both couples were staying. Denise and I met up with the four of them in the hotel lobby. I cannot even tell you exactly what was all said; I just know that seeing Steve for the first time felt, for lack of a better term, familiar. It seemed like I had always known him—like he had been a part of us, and this was normal. And Steve's wife, Melody, was just a dream. Both were so nice and sweet and completely lovable.

I have been told that our family, when all together, can be a little overwhelming, but it was such a pleasure to find them right in the middle of the teasing and cutting up. That is not always an easy thing to do. We had a wonderful conversation that stretched into dinner just getting to know each other. I was so happy to tell my parents about the day we had spent together and what a delight Steve and Melody were.

When the day finally arrived for Steve and Dad to meet face-to-face, everyone was a little nervous. My husband, John, was driving us all to the restaurant. Mom and Dad were both uncharacteristically quiet during the ride. I asked Mom if she was okay, and she admitted she had butterflies in her stomach. Dad admitted aloud that he did, too. This surprised me because Dad does not usually admit to such weaknesses. John dropped us in front of the restaurant while he went to park the car. I was standing beside Dad as Steve was walking across the parking lot toward us. I leaned over to Dad and whispered to him, *"He looks like Uncle Philip, doesn't he?"*

Dad looked at me with a big smile on his face and said, *"He really does!"*

Now that Dad is gone, that is one of the pictures of him that I will always carry in my mind and in my heart—that look of true happiness.

CHAPTER 41

Debra

I am Steve's next-to-the-youngest sister, Debra. I was not going to contribute to this story because I do not readily share my feelings and I am more on the quiet side. The more I read of Steve's writings, though, I thought I might lend some of my perspective to the story.

I was on vacation in Florida when my sister, Denise, called and told Cheryl and me about Steve. I still remember that call so vividly and the mixed feelings that ranged between thinking, *"It can't be real"*, but also feeling excited that I could have another sibling.

Let me back up for a minute and tell you about my family. They are amazing. We love each other completely and without fail. My siblings are my best friends. My dad was the disciplinarian, but he showed us love with physical things. It was not until he got older that he actually started saying that he loved us, but we always knew he did. My mom is the lovey, hugging kind of mom who always makes us know we are loved. Now back to my story.

I was not able to meet Steve and Melody when all the family first met them because I was traveling for work. In fact, I did not get to meet Steve and Melody until my father's funeral, but the moment I saw him, it felt like I had always known him. It was a very strange, yet calming feeling. *That is my brother!* It was an automatic feeling of love. Melody also felt like family, and it is so wonderful that they never acted like visitors; they seemed just to fit right into us.

I now have my oldest brother, Steve; my oldest sister, Denise; my youngest brother, Chuck; my older sister, Cheryl; and my youngest sister, Janel. Not to mention I now have another nephew and great-nephew! What a delight.

On top of this joyous occasion of meeting my new brother, there is also an underlying sadness and, I hate to say it, also anger. I feel cheated that Steve was not told about his real father when his search first began. I feel anger toward his mother that he was not told much sooner so that he could have decided for himself if he wanted to pursue a relationship with us. I feel anger that he did not have more time to get to know our father, and that my father was cheated out of getting to know Steve.

Now that I have had more time with Steve, I enjoy just watching him with his little quirks that were the same as my father's. Who would have known just how much he would be like Dad? I feel like my father is still with us. It makes me smile to see Steve roll his soda bottle top around or when he smooths out the table in front of him.

We are still a strong loving family who has embraced our new family members and will continue to do so hopefully long into the future.

CHAPTER 42

Janel

I am the youngest of Steve's sisters, Janel. I had four siblings prior to learning about Steve. The five of us have always been close, but not always on the best of terms. Even when we are fussing at each other, we will still drop everything to help when another sibling needs us.

When I received a phone call in July 2017 from my sister, Cheryl, it seemed like any other call to catch up on our lives. It turned out to be a very special and life altering phone call, though. Cheryl explained to me about her phone call with our sister, Denise, and that we have a brother we never knew about. After quite a few shocking expletives, she relayed to me some of Steve's journey to find us.

My first reaction was anger at Steve's mother for not giving him the information sooner and telling our father. It was an automatic reaction that I later thought better of.

At first, I was shocked that I had a new brother. After I got off the phone, I really digested the information Cheryl had revealed to me. It was at that time when I realized I was not that surprised after all. Because our father had dated other people before meeting my mother at age twenty-four, a missing sibling was a possibility even though it had been the 1950s. Truthfully, the only thing I focused on, or cared about, was that Steve's conception happened years before my parents met and married. It would have been more difficult, but possible, to accept had it happened during my parents' marriage.

On the following Sunday, all five of the original siblings had a conference call with Steve and his wife, Melody. It did not feel like we were on the phone for ninety minutes, but we were. The second I heard his and Melody's voices, I knew they were part of our family. I had not even met them in person yet, but it did not matter. The conversation went by as if we had all known each other our whole lives.

In the following weeks, Steve and I made plans for him and Melody to make a trip to Kansas to visit my family in September. However, before his trip to Kansas, we all got the call that our dad had died. I flew to Georgia for the funeral and met Steve and Melody for the first time at the funeral home. No one even had to tell me that the man standing in the foyer at the funeral home was Steve because he was virtually an identical twin to Dad's brother, Uncle Philip. I hugged Steve and Melody, and it was as if I had always known them. They were our family.

Epilogue

When I started writing this story in the fall of 2017, my mother was alive and residing in Des Moines, Iowa, with my sister, Janelle. Mom was able to fill in the many gaps I came across as I initially researched the DNA results obtained from the testing service. While the help she provided was given begrudgingly at first, she eventually began answering all my questions more freely regardless of embarrassment or personal toll. I would have ultimately arrived at the same conclusions regarding my DNA family history; however, it would have taken a lot longer and likely ended with no firsthand acknowledgements. I am inclined to believe I would have missed many important moments for myself with the Weeks family over the past year as well.

I pass along my thanks to her in memoriam now, as Mom passed away in early April 2018, almost two years to the day of my dad, Moe's, passing. I was able to tell her many things about the Weeks family before her passing and give her my very personal thanks for being so truthful in the end. For the remainder of my life, I will have the knowledge she was ultimately happy that I had found and positively connected with my biological father's family.

I cannot say for sure what her expectation for my actions would have been when she finally broke the truth to me about Chuck Sr. in July 2017. I am positive her first hope was I would not pursue the connection. As I have stated earlier in the story, I have a dad. During one of the early conversations after the admission, she informed me that the reason she and Dad never told me (or Kerry) about our fathers was twofold. Moe wanted us to believe that we were his children, and he never knew about Chuck Sr. Moe truly believed

I was Sonny Kreider's son and Kerry's full sibling until the day he passed.

During my last meeting with Mom while visiting Des Moines in mid-March 2018 before her passing in early April, she sat alone with me and offered her apologies for the years of mistruths and secrets. She said she had never told another soul about my true biological father because it was her burden to bear. It was almost as though she had carried the weight as a punishment for her early adult years of reckless behaviors. The look on her face told me she was relieved to share and shed that secret finally and forever. It also confirmed what Melody and I had long suspected as we discussed the various information gleaned during the exhaustive research.

Mom offered many apologies about the events from my childhood that were less than idyllic. There was discussion about many topics for which she had regrets for her actions or inactions. I did my best to relieve her concerns and told her there was no more time to be sorrowful. I explained that we children no longer held any ill will about our growing years. Time heals most wounds. Bad experiences are forgotten and forgiven. Nobody has time to wallow in past actions or unpleasantness. We are living forward, and I hope I eased her burdens.

When I started looking into Chuck Sr. and came across the answers to his whereabouts so quickly, Mom never really had time to assess what impact her less-than-thrilled initial responses about my findings would have on me. I am sure her cautious replies during my attempts at keeping her informed of my progress added to my negative perception of her intentions. It may also have had significant bearing on my distrust of the information she provided until I could corroborate with any other source. I am grateful to have rebuilt a large portion of that trust during the past year.

During some very deep and personal conversations Janelle and I had as we hashed out Mom's life in preparation for her funeral, Janelle relayed to me about many a discussion she had with Mom relating to my DNA activities and family search. I was surprised to find out Mom was, at first, jealous that the Weeks family had welcomed me with such open arms. I, however, had expressed to her my pleasure and amazement about the Weeks family many times, including as recently as the last visit we made to Des Moines just three weeks prior to her passing. My positive reports and enthusiasm about the Weeks family is what changed her perspective from jealousy to happiness.

Mom came to understand that I had no intentions, nor was it even a remote possibility, to cut her or my sisters out of my life as I become more involved with my Weeks family. This was a real concern she apparently harbored and had expressed to Janelle on more than one occasion.

To illustrate how I went about keeping her involved in my life, I told Janelle that Chuck had expressed an interest in meeting her because she was so important to me. Janelle gave essentially the same message to me. She was just as interested in meeting all of them and stated that the Weeks family is her family because they are also mine. As we have always felt, what is important to each of us is important to both of us.

Many events have occurred over my lifetime that have shaped the individual I am today. I would be foolish to think that any change of circumstance at any time of my life would not have an impact on my current situations. It is within reason to believe that this outcome could have been very different. I cannot guess what the impact to me may have been had the knowledge been brought forth earlier in my life. We cannot know what might have happened from either my side or the Weeks side.

We must not get into the speculative realm of the could-have, would-have, might-have, or should-have thoughts. We can only be thankful for where we are now and never lament our past; rather, we should use it to build the foundation for goodness moving forward. As Melody is fond of saying, "Timing is everything." For this story, for my life story, for my family story, this is the time.

If there is a master plan out there in the world of fate, this journey has turned into a juggernaut traveling the correct path for my future endeavors. I have a wonderful original family and a wonderful new family, which simply equates to having a wonderful family to share life with as we continue moving forward.

My Journey

- I lived my first nineteen years believing my name was Steven James Vermeulen.
- I was led to believe my name was Steven James Kreider.
- I legally changed my name to Steven James Vermeulen in 1998.
- My birth certificate father is Melvin Lee (Sonny) Kreider (passed 2006).
- My birth father is Charles Edward Weeks Sr. (passed 2017).
- My step-father is Morris Charles Vermeulen (passed 2016).
- My mother is Constance Louise Vermeulen (passed 2018).
- My step-mother is Ellon Louise Weeks.

My Siblings

- A sister, Kerry Kreider (born 1954, passed 2002).
- I am second-oldest sibling among the nine (born 1956).
- A sister, Janelle Ballard (born 1957).
- A sister, Denise Weeks Lovell (born 1961).
- A brother, Charles Weeks Jr. (born 1962).
- A sister, Brenda Cole (born 1962).
- A sister, Cheryl Oncay (born 1963).
- A sister, Debra Mullis (born 1965).
- A sister, Janel Harder (born 1968).

Submitting Your DNA

While I was very fortunate that my birth father, his wife, and all five of my new siblings were accepting of me and welcomed me into their family instantly, I know of others who have not been as lucky and have been rejected by some of their close family matches. Not being accepting of unexpected family and not taking a moment to get to know them often means someone is cheating himself or herself out of a great relationship with a great person.

Here are a few tips Melody and I have learned along the way, and things you might want to think about if you decide to take your own DNA journey:

- Be as certain as you can be that you are completely prepared to find out what you find out. Be open to and accepting of your DNA results—the good, the bad, the sad, the disappointing, and (perhaps most importantly) the unexpected.
- If an unexpected close family match reaches out to you, be accepting, honest, and forthcoming with information about yourself and open-minded to information about them.
- Do not cheat yourself out of a relationship with someone because you fear judgement.
- If you are a male and have submitted your DNA to a registry, be ready and willing to accept that it might be a child who finds you or you them. Any man who has ever had unprotected sex, regardless of the length of a relationship, could very well have fathered a child and never known.
- DNA matching is becoming much more commonplace. Babies born decades ago and perhaps not raised by one or either

birth parent understandably want to connect with family they have just discovered through DNA testing. It is a very real possibility that one of those parents may have had no idea that a child of theirs ever existed, as was the case with me.
- If you reach out to a close family match and find that your existence is something that person may not have shared with a husband, wife, children, or others in his or her life, give that person the time he or she needs to open the discovery discussion with their loved ones. Hopefully they will have faith that the important people in their lives will be understanding and supportive of decisions made years earlier.
- Remember that everyone has a past, and we have all made choices using the best information we had at the time. We might make different choices today.
- If a close family match resists your initial attempts to communicate, be prepared for the possibility that the person may never be receptive because they may fear the revelation of your existence will have a major impact on them or an existing family dynamic. If you are fortunate enough to establish new family relationships, nurture them for as long as you have them. While life may be good before DNA testing, it can be even more so if DNA matches lead to new and lasting family relationships.
- Lastly, consider submitting your DNA to more than just one site. Doing so will greatly increase the number of family matches. I initially submitted to just one service and submitted to a second one within a few months. This not only widened my results, it also confirmed results I had already gotten.

There are several DNA registries to choose from. All of them frequently offer DNA kits at a discount, so it does not have to cost you a small fortune to purchase and submit DNA to several. In addition, these registries do not share results between them, which makes being in multiple registries a good idea.

The Moral of This Story

My new family should be held up as the *perfect* example of how to welcome new—albeit unexpected—family members. Not a single parent, sibling, niece, nephew, aunt, uncle, or family friend has shown Melody and me anything but a genuinely warm welcome, and for that, we are incredibly grateful. Our only regret is that we did not know about them sooner.

While it would be easy to feel cheated and hold a grudge against some for not being forthcoming with the truth years ago, it seems like a waste of time and energy. Instead, we plan to make the most of the years ahead and set about making new memories with our new family and putting any negative thoughts or feelings away; they serve no purpose. At the end of the day, the positives about this journey far outweigh any negatives, and I am a lucky man indeed.

In Conclusion

I must give thanks to my wife, Melody, and everyone in my family who contributed to this story. Denise's suggestion last year that I should write a book planted the notion in my head. After months of rewrites and editing and endless support and encouragement from so many, here it is. This would not have been possible without my family's total support and their willingness to share their thoughts and personal feelings freely and openly.

The past year has been quite the learning experience. I endured my share of disappointments and frustrations during my forty-plus-year search for answers to a family I thought existed. There were many times when I considered stopping. I am so grateful, however, to have kept the search alive because my perseverance led me to an awesome new family. My life was good before, but it is even better now that my search is over. My hope for others who decide to embark on this same journey is that they achieve the same wonderful outcome I did. You deserve it, and I wish you all the luck in the world!

Index

A Father & Family Are Found 33
After 61 Years, Father & Son Meet at Last 76
A Sibling Responds 64
Cheryl 122
Chuck 113
Collateral Damage? 93
Dad, Is That You? 59
Debra 126
Denise 107
Ellon 105
Family Fellowship & Future Plans 84
Honoring a Life Well Lived 81
I Ask Myself More Questions 62
I Follow the Bread Crumbs 49
I'm Getting Close 44
In Conclusion 141
I Think I Found My Brother 35
Janel 128
Janelle 102
Meeting Time Has Arrived! 73
Melody 98
My Early Years 1
My Family Shares Their Perspectives 97
My First Taste of Real Freedom 19
My High School Years 16
My Journey 134
My Name Is What? 26
My Pre-teen & Early Teen Years 7
My Search Begins 29

My Siblings 135
New Family, Old Traditions 95
Oh No ... Surely Not ☹ 79
Our Family Business Forms 13
Positive Notes 89
Questions, Questions, Questions 52
Spitting In a Tube 37
Steven, We Need to Talk 22
Steven, We Need to Talk (again) 46
Submitting Your DNA 137
The Best "Surprise" Family 91
The Moral of This Story 139
The Siblings Are Gathered 87
Two DNA Services Agree 88
We Begin Telling Friends & Family 66
Weeks? 41
We Must Get Together 70
When Ignorance & Intolerance Came Calling 10
Wrestling with Answers 56

About the Author

Steve is a son, brother, father, grandfather, and husband. He and Melody currently reside in Cary, North Carolina.